DATE DUE

~~NO20'00~~			
~~DE11'00~~			
~~DE20'00~~			
~~NO13'00~~			
MY22'03			
~~MR2~~			
~~AP17'04~~			
FE 9'06			

THEORIES OF
MORAL DEVELOPMENT

THEORIES OF MORAL DEVELOPMENT

Second Edition

By

JOHN MARTIN RICH, Ph.D.

The University of Texas at Austin

JOSEPH L. DeVITIS, Ph.D.

State University of New York at Binghamton

CHARLES C THOMAS • PUBLISHER

Springfield • Illinois • U.S.A.

Distributed Throughout the World by

CHARLES C THOMAS • PUBLISHER
2600 South First Street
Springfield, Illinois 62794-9265

© *1994 by* CHARLES C THOMAS • PUBLISHER

ISBN 0-398-05924-1

Library of Congress Catalog Card Number: 94-21565

First Edition, 1985
Second Edition, 1994

With THOMAS BOOKS *careful attention is given to all details of manufacturing
and design. It is the Publisher's desire to present books that are satisfactory as to their
physical qualities and artistic possibilities and appropriate for their particular use.*
THOMAS BOOKS *will be true to those laws of quality that assure a good name
and good will.*

Printed in the United States of America
SC-R-3

Library of Congress Cataloging-in-Publication Data

Rich, John Martin.
    Theories of moral development / by John Martin Rich, Joseph L.
DeVitis. — 2nd ed.
        p.   cm.
    Includes bibliographical references and index.
    ISBN 0-398-05924-1
    1. Moral Development.   I. DeVitis, Joseph L.   II. Title.
BF723.M54R53   1994
155.2'5 — dc20   94-21565
                                                                CIP

PREFACE AND ACKNOWLEDGMENTS

This book represents the authors' conviction that interpretive, normative, and critical perspectives be brought to bear in the analysis of moral development theory. From the book's inception, the purpose has been to set the stage for an introductory meeting ground that might engage those who are interested in reconciling the separate paths often taken by students in psychology, education, philosophy, and social criticism. Thus the objective is to bring together these divergent strands in moral development theory; consequently, thinkers whose contributions to moral development theory have been neglected are accorded more complete treatment.

The First Edition was selected as one of *Choice* magazine's 1985–86 Outstanding Academic Books and Nonprint Materials. This edition uses the same organization as the First Edition, but has added presentations and evaluations of social learning theory, hermeneutics and moral action, empathy and social cognition, cross-cultural human development, and psychosocial theory. In addition, a bibliography and a concluding chapter are provided along with other changes and updated material.

John Martin Rich did the research and writing of the Second Edition, as Joseph L. DeVitis was involved in another major project. DeVitis, however, did discuss the project, read and commented on the manuscript. I have profited considerably from criticisms, recommendations, and insights from numerous reviews of the First Edition. I wish to thank Payne Thomas for his interest in a Second Edition and his encouragement in the project, and Becca Maxwell for her accurate and efficient word processing.

CONTENTS

THEORIES OF
MORAL DEVELOPMENT

Chapter 1

MORAL DEVELOPMENT IN EDUCATION AND PSYCHOLOGY: AN OVERVIEW

M ORAL development was cited as a primary responsibility for public schools by more than two-thirds of the respondents to Gallup
polls on education. At the same time, psychologists and other mental
health practitioners have been perplexed about what constitutes "moral
development" and how descriptions and explanations of it can contribute to a harmonizing of individual needs and societal pressures. Recent
crises, from the civil rights movement in the 1960s through issues raised
by the fundamentalists today, have served to muddle in the public mind
such distinctions as morals, manners, mores, and ethics. Belief systems
do not clarify what is actually entailed in moral decision and "moral
development." That is to say, popular crises in morality have tended to
divert energies away from more critical and fundamental inquiry into
human nature, both human capabilities and limitations. Any fair assessment of moral accountability requires that the human being be capable
of doing that for which he is judged.

It is for this reason that scholars and practitioners need to retrieve,
elucidate, and analyze critically those systematic, theoretical syntheses of
moral development that are already available and to evaluate whether
these alternatives offer a way out of current confusion about moral
decision making. By becoming clearer about foundational bases for
morality, both the professional educator and mental health practitioner
will be able to achieve a firmer grasp, or conceptual handle, on those
issues which seem to be so important, but confusing, to the lay public. As
theories of moral development provide new insights, opportunities
improve for the discovery of new ideas about morality. This is more the
case when a consensual body of knowledge about moral development is
made available to both lay and professional audiences so that they can
engage in dialogue.

Most textbooks limit themselves to certain major models of moral

3

development, especially the cognitive-structural psychology of Piaget and Kohlberg. While this is an important approach and will be treated herein, what is missing is a more comprehensive treatment of competing theories. Thus this book affords a comprehensive treatment and elaboration of *competing options* in moral development as generated by a host of other psychological theories. It therefore relates different universes of discourse about moral development so that professionals and laypersons alike will be able to articulate and refine moral issues out of *diverse* frameworks.

A LOOK AHEAD

The introductory chapter clarifies key terms and lays the background for different theories of moral development. Emile Durkheim is introduced because many developmental theorists either build upon or attempt to move around his theories.

Chapter 2 will survey competing models from various schools of thought on the initial origins of morality in childhood: Freud's psychoanalytical model; Alfred Adler's views from Individual Psychology; Jung's neo-analytical contributions; Albert Bandura's social learning theory; and Piaget's very influential cognitive-structural approach.

Chapter 3 includes Erik H. Erikson's sociocultural synthesis, particularly the problem of "identity" crisis; Robert J. Havighurst's description of "developmental tasks," which seem to be especially relevant to adolescent life adjustment; Martin J. Packer's studies of hermeneutics and moral action; and Martin L. Hoffman's research on empathy and social cognition.

Chapter 4 covers the explicit body of data-based research that has focused on knowledge about how higher education affects or does not affect moral development. Surveyed here will be such diverse ideas as Philip E. Jacob's analysis of value change in college; Arthur Chickering on education and integrity; William Perry's study of growth and commitment in college; Douglas Heath's model of maturing; and Kenneth Keniston on student radicals and the alienated and uncommitted.

Chapter 5 presents a panoramic view, drawn from multiple sources, of lifelong patterns and detours (some presumably invariant, others presumably changeable) that stem from a growing body of research. Included here are Lawrence Kohlberg's dominant paradigm of a universal, hierarchical form of moral development; Carol Gilligan's counter-paradigm of women's moral growth; Jane Loevinger's "milestones of development," which adapts ego-psychology to different life stages; Daniel Levinson's focus on men's problems of work, love, security, and needs for continuous reassessment and enrichment; James Fowler's studies of faith and development in the life cycle; Abram Kardiner's studies of basic personality structure and John W. Berry's ecological approach that offer needed cross-cultural models; and William M. Kurtines' psychosocial theory that views human behavior as rule governed and seeks a more comprehensive theory than either Piaget or Kohlberg.

The final chapter addresses certain issues pertinent to all moral development theories: pluralism and heterogeneity of the field; theory development; determinism and nondeterminism; and morality and immorality.

KEY TERMS

Certain key terms which may appear frequently should be clarified. Whenever a thinker coins his own definition that is at odds with those presented below, then this stipulative definition will be indicated at the appropriate point.

Morality, first of all, should be distinguished from manners and mores. *Manners* are concerned with matters of taste and etiquette based on prudential judgments. Such judgments concern circumspection, shrewdness, or wiseness in judgments about practical affairs. Although one's prudential judgments and moral judgments will occasionally coincide, they frequently may differ. One may decide to do something because it will help one to advance, gain control over something or someone, or for financial gain even though the morality of the act may be questionable. Telling the truth may be the moral thing to do, but to do so may impede one's professional advancement in a certain situation; therefore, the individual may find it prudent to distort, be evasive, or lie.

By *mores* is meant the fixed morally-binding customs of a particular group. Mores vary considerably cross-culturally and throughout human history, ranging from the noblest behavior to the approval of slavery, infanticide, burning infidels at the stake, genocide, and other practices.

In contrast, *morality* is a system of conduct based on moral principles. That which is *moral*, therefore, relates to principles of right conduct in behavior; the behavior complies with accepted principles of what is considered right, virtuous or just. To say that a certain act is immoral means that it is unvirtuous or contrary to morality because it does not conform to principles of right conduct.

Two cognate terms should be considered: *amoral* and *nonmoral.* Amoral has more than one meaning insofar as it may refer to someone who is indifferent to or does not care to abide by moral codes. Or it may refer to someone who lacks moral sensibility, such as infants, because of immaturity. It may also be equated with nonmoral, an act which is neither moral nor immoral, such as a decision to buy a particular tie.

The study of the nature of morality consists of two major approaches: the scientific and the philosophical. The scientific utilizes social and behavioral science methodology to uncover how people actually behave and what they believe about morality. The philosophical approach, in contrast, is known as *ethics,* which is a study of the nature of morality and moral acts. Ethics is divided into normative ethics and metaethics. Normative ethics is concerned with what people ought to do (Should one always tell the truth?) and with systems of ethics (Epicureanism, Stoicism, Kantianism, utilitarianism, etc.). Metaethics analyzes ethical language and the justification of ethical inquiry and judgments.

The term, *development,* refers to progressive and continuous changes in the organism from birth to death. These changes can include changes in the shape and integration of bodily parts into functional parts; and intellectual, social, emotional, or moral development that may occur at different periods of an individual's life. These periods can be conveniently divided into infancy, childhood, adolescence, young adulthood, middle age, and old age (however, different theories may divide or combine them differently).

Development can be ascribed to the interaction of the organism and the environment in which both learned behavior and heredity are operative. Though heredity may include physical characteristics (hair and eye color, hair distribution, etc.), maturation is of greater interest in developmental studies. By *maturation* is meant that part of the development process that can be attributed to heredity or is species-specific behavior, such as walking.

Moral development refers to growth of the individual's ability to distinguish right from wrong, to develop a system of ethical values, and to learn to act morally. A moral development theory explains how individuals develop morally. A *theory* is a body of principles used to explain phenomena. Related is the term *moral education,* which refers to instruction in moral rules of conduct for the purpose of developing good character traits and ethical behavior. Such instruction may be systematically planned (as with moral education programs in churches and schools) or unplanned (as a parent reprimanding her offspring for immoral behavior).

The process of socialization relative to both moral development and education should be distinguished because moral development occurs not only through maturation and education but socialization as well. *Socialization* is the process by which the individual becomes inculcated with societal values and acquires appropriate social roles. It involves the internalization of social norms as individuals guide their own actions to comply with the expectations of others. Socialization can be divided into three stages: the primary stage of socializing the young child in the family; the secondary stage in school; and third stage of adult socialization (as husband or wife, parent, and employee).

Moral development theory, although drawing upon the socialization process, also emphasizes maturation, growth, developmental stages, and the emergence of different cognitive and moral abilities. By including maturation, moral development theory studies the organism, including its biological basis, which is usually absent from socialization considerations. Socialization explanations also do not account for the processes of growth by which the individual is able to master more complex tasks or more sophisticated interpersonal relations.

In contrast, *education* is a generic term that refers to an intentional process that has objectives, content, and outcomes and takes place both in educational institutions and informal settings. Education is designed not only to transmit knowledge and the cultural heritage but to improve individuals by engaging their thinking, feeling, and action. Objectives refer to what one hopes to achieve in the process; the content is what is taught, and the outcomes are what is actually achieved. That objectives are stipulated shows that the process is intentional and pre-planned, not accidental or inadvertent (as in the case of some learning).

What is the difference, then, between socialization and education? One of the chief tasks of socialization is the learning of roles (son, daughter, friend, student, and so on). Thus, one learns appropriate roles for his age, sex, social class, and personal responsibilities. Socialization processes instill proper social rules and thereby help preserve social institutions. Though schools and other institutions and agencies engage in socialization, it is a primary activity of the family. Education, on the other hand, is usually designed to develop new ideas and improve society by providing students with requisite knowledge and reflective abilities. This is less true in the early grades in which the acquisition of basic skills and a rudimentary knowledge of the cultural heritage are emphasized.

Certain issues are raised in the forthcoming analysis of different theories:

(1) the cognitive-structural grounds for judging what one should do in moral dilemma situations;

(2) the degree of consistency between ethical values and moral action;

(3) the degree of consistency between cognitive-structural ways of making meaning of a system of ethical values and moral action;

(4) the psychosocial issues that need resolution in order for a person to reason and/or act morally;

(5) the role of the social context in determining the nature of right and wrong and in hindering or assisting moral action.[1]

INDIVIDUAL AUTONOMY AND SOCIAL STABILITY

Societies are interested in maintaining themselves over extended time periods and preserving their cultural heritage. At the same time, most societies seek to improve themselves—promote greater economic growth, advancements in technology, better international relations, higher educational standards, or in some other way. Certain forms of independence and autonomy are needed among citizens to enjoy the creativity to effect these improvements. Not all changes, however, are improvements or reforms, and some reforms may threaten older values and traditions. Thus, a tension arises between individual autonomy and social stability.

One explanation for how stability is maintained in society is based on a social disorganization theory.[2] A social system is organized through a consistent set of norms and values that fosters orderly and predictable social action among its members. Leaders of society try to foster a normative consensus. Social disorganization results whenever orderly social interaction breaks down and normative consensus fails to be achieved. Disorganization stems from anomie (a state of normlessness) or a lack of consensus on norms. Whenever disorganization and anomie occur, devi-

---

[1]Drawn from a review of this book's first edition by Robert F. Rodgers. *Journal of Higher Education,* 57, 554, September 1986.

[2]Examples of the social disorganization theory: Merton, Robert K.: *Social Theory and Social Structure,* Glencoe, Ill., Free Press, 1957; Cohen, Albert K., *Deviance and Control.* Englewood Cliffs, N.J., Prentice Hall, 1966; and McGee, Reece, *Social Disorganization in America,* San Francisco, Chandler, 1962.

ant behavior is likely to result; and as disorganization grows, deviance and violence increase. Social disorganization is expressed in inadequate institutionalization of goals, inappropriate procedures for achieving goals, weakened social control, and shifting population.

Thus the tasks for avoiding social disorganization are to create a normative consensus, to develop compelling goals and consistent procedures for achieving them, and to institute effective socialization practices.

Each individual who strives for independence will not likely become independent without developing certain skills and competencies that are created within various authority patterns. In other words, the authority of the home and school become models for the meaning of one's search for independence. The process of becoming independent also involves assuming some of the different authority types for oneself, to become increasingly one's own authority and, as a young adult's new responsibilities should call for it (as when one becomes a parent or a teacher), to play the appropriate authority-type role to the young of the next generation.

Angyal has postulated an approach which involves two different but complementary orientations.[3] One is that the organism tends to strive for increased autonomy, even though there are heteronomous influences that decrease it. According to this theory, the life process is characterized by two components: autonomy and heteronomy, or self-government and government from outside.

Angyal suggests that there can be not only a lack of autonomy (one of the characteristics of neurotic living) but an excess of autonomous striving. A lack of autonomy is manifested in excessive conformism, inability to form independent judgments or disagree with anyone, and dependence upon others far in excess of necessity.

But less widely recognized is excessive autonomous striving. Here the characteristic behavior includes extreme resentment and rejection of the influence of others, intolerance and rebelliousness, and the need to test continually or "prove" oneself by acts designed to show competency or mastery.[4] Excessive autonomous striving, frequently the pattern of adolescents and adults who are unsure of their mastery over their environment, should not be confused with healthy forms of autonomy.

Angyal calls the healthy form of heteronomy *homonomy.* "The person behaves as if he were seeking a place for himself in a larger unit of which

---

[3]Angyal, Andras: *Neurosis and Treatment: A Holistic Approach.* New York, Wiley, 1965.
[4]Ibid., p. 12.

he strives to become a part."[5] One cannot master the environment by force or violence, but must understand and comply with environmental laws, which is to adopt a homonomous attitude. Thus autonomy and homonomy, for Angyal, are complementary orientations that have their norms in healthy expression.

These complementary orientations can also be found in Riesman's interpretation of the autonomous person as one who is capable of conforming to societal norms but free to choose whether or not to conform; he is less the creature of circumstance than other characterological types, such as "tradition-directed," "inner-directed," and "other-directed" persons.[6]

Thus the choices in human development, for Angyal and Riesman, are to seek complementary orientations, or to emphasize either autonomy or social stability. Stability would be maintained by adopting a homonomous attitude and instituting other measures (mentioned above) to avert social disorganization. Whereas for autonomy, "the individual increasingly comes to feel," according to Rogers, "that the locus of evaluation lies within himself."[7] Other choices, in addition to those previously stated, will be developed in subsequent chapters.

DURKHEIM'S PARADIGM

Perhaps the most classic attempt to weigh the seemingly competing interests of social stability and individual autonomy can be found in the pioneering work of the French sociologist Emile Durkheim (1858–1916). Indeed, his seminal effort to articulate these alternative claims builds a basis for analysis in moral development which later theorists would have to attack head on, or at least acknowledge, in their own attempts to construct "better bridges" for ethical argumentation. Unfortunately, Durkheim has not received the wide attention that he deserves. For that reason, and for the purpose of clarifying subsequent models of moral development, Durkheim's original paradigm will be analyzed and discussed in some detail.

According to Durkheim, there are three basic elements in the internal-

---

[5]Ibid., p. 15.

[6]Riesman, D., Glazer, N., and Denney, R.: *The Lonely Crowd.* New Haven, Yale, 1952.

[7]Rogers, Carl: *On Becoming a Person.* Boston: Houghton Mifflin, 1961, p. 119.

ization of moral values: (1) "the spirit of authority and discipline"; (2) "attachment to social groups"; and (3) "autonomy," or self-determination.

Durkheim speaks of authority and discipline as moral imperatives which "perform an important function in forming character and personality in general."[8] He posits authority and discipline as essential because of their capacity for restraint, allowing sentient human beings to "contain our passions, our desires, our habits, and subject them to law."[9] Thus, without discipline, man would be a slave to impulse and, as a consequence, be neither free nor happy. At the same time, discipline promotes its own self-regulating patterns of conduct and cooperation which make for a kind of "social glue" without which human organization would be impossible. Taken together, then, authority and discipline permit us to safeguard social stability and to establish possibilities for individual autonomy. For Durkheim, moral rules and human liberties are not viewed as exclusive or antithetical terms, but as part of concrete social practice and specific social context.

Pedagogically, it becomes the function of the educator to inculcate those habits of conduct, those norms and rules, which serve to integrate the child into the stable, ongoing rhythms of social reality. Indeed, Durkheim implies that discipline itself is a moral end in that it mediates the child's initial egoism.

In this regard, some observers have accused Durkheim of failing to distinguish "socialization" from "education."[10] Simply given his emphasis on authority and discipline, socialization would appear to be Durkheim's chief intention. However, as will be pointed out subsequently, he was also vitally interested in education *qua* education.

The second main feature of Durkheim's moral paradigm lies in the individual's attachment to the group. In his very first book, *The Division of Labor* (1893), Durkheim presages his allegiance to the social framework of all morality: "Let social life disappear and moral life will

---

[8]Durkheim, Emile: *Moral Education: A Study in the Theory and Application of the Sociology of Knowledge* (1925), Everett K. Wilson and Herman Schnurer (Tr.). New York, Free Press, 1961, p. 46.

[9]*Ibid.*

[10]"Socialization" can be viewed as "the process by which an individual acquires the knowledge, skills, and behavior that will make him an adequate member of society. . . . One of the chief tasks in socialization is the learning of roles. . . . Socialization processes instill proper social rules and thereby help preserve social institutions. Education, on the other hand, is usually designed to change and improve individuals and society by providing requisite knowledge and reflective abilities." Rich, John Martin: *Discipline and Authority in School and Family.* Lexington, Lexington Books, 1982, pp. 115, 134.

disappear with it, since it would no longer have any objective."[11] In large measure, Durkheim is also foreshadowing later social milieu theorists such as George Herbert Mead in his insistence on identifying the moral life as moving beyond the realm of the "I" to that of the "We." Like some of these subsequent thinkers, Durkheim couches his terms in an evolutionary context:

> Family, nation, and humanity represent different phases of our social and moral evolution, stages that prepare for, and build upon, one another. . . . Just as each has its part to play in historical development, they mutually complement each other in the present.[12]

During Durkheim's lifetime, the contemporary milieu in France and other Western societies exhibited tendencies toward normlessness or a lack of fixedness in moral authority (what Durkheim terms "anomie"), precarious signposts of imbalance in social attachment. These imbalances are symptomatic of what Durkheim calls "excessive individualism" or "excessive integration," both of which result, he claims, in abnormal increases in suicide:[13]

> Both suicidal types are defined in terms of *attachment* to collectively shared moral concepts, egoistic suicide being due to insufficient attachment to shared moral beliefs and altruistic suicide being the result of excessive solidarity with, and devotion to, group ends.[14]

Durkheim's classic study of suicide casts in bold relief the need to balance social stability with growth in individual autonomy if humankind is to survive and overcome conditions of personal and institutional disorganization.

The third component in Durkheim's moral paradigm, autonomy and self-determination, shows most clearly how he weds the competing demands for solidarity and individuality. According to most modern ethical theories, especially since Immanuel Kant, action and behavior cannot be judged "moral" unless it is accompanied by some substantial degree of "autonomous" reflection on the part of the moral actor. That is to say, the moral agent must be aware of, and understand, those rules of conduct which surround his/her moral decision making. It is for this

---

[11]Durkheim, Emile: *The Division of Labor* (1893), George Simpson (Tr.). New York, Macmillan, 1933, p. 399.

[12]*Ibid.*

[13]Durkheim, Emile: *Suicide: A Study in Sociology* (1897), J.A. Spaulding and George Simpson (Tr.). New York, Free Press, 1952.

[14]Wellwork, Ernest: *Durkheim: Morality and Milieu.* Cambridge, Harvard U.P., 1972, pp. 48–49.

reason that Durkheim attempts to liberate man from "direct dependence on things" by a form of concerted, rational, and scientific investigation of the external data around him:

> We fashion [autonomy]...ourselves to the extent that we achieve a more complete knowledge of things. [Autonomy] does not imply that the human being, in any of his aspects, escapes the world and its laws.... But, if in some measure we are the products of things, we can, through science, use our understanding to control both the things that exert an influence upon us and this influence itself. In this way, we again become our master.[15]

Consequently, educators do not merely inculcate habits of conduct; they also instill in students an understanding of social reality which will enable them to shape their moral destiny. However, it should be noted once again that Durkheim never makes morality an entity unto itself or solely an instrument of individual human creation. Man's moral actions always derive from the social world: "It is a dangerous illusion to imagine that morality is a personal artifact; and that consequently we have it completely under our control."[16]

In a briefer section of his *Moral Education,* Durkheim traces several models of personality which resemble some modern prototypes in the literature of social and psychological theory. He postulates that these models are representative of "two extreme and opposed types in men's moral character." The first, more dominant, type he characterizes as being "sensitive to the rule," i.e., those persons in society who are predisposed to authority and discipline. This moral personality is happiest when duty, couched in rationality, can be executed properly (Durkheim cites the philosopher Kant as a prototypal example). The second personality type is more apt to be recognizable for its propensity to "spend" itself by an "outward expansiveness." More bound by the emotions, these individuals like to help others and do not act strictly by reason or logic. In this instance, Durkheim is already introducing a personality type which would later be described in various other terms by future psychologists and social theorists.[17]

Echoing Max Weber, Durkheim also speaks of "charismatic" figures

---

[15]Durkheim, Emile: *Moral Education,* pp. 114, 119.

[16]*Ibid.*

[17]For example, as someone imbued with "social interest" by Alfred Adler; as an "extrovert" by Carl Jung; and as an "other-directed" person by David Riesman. Similarly, Durkheim's "sensitive-to-the-rule" types seem to parallel Jung's "introverts" and Riesman's "inner-directed" figures. For Adler, such personalities might be viewed as "lacking in social interest."

who influence cold social facts and the inevitable movement of history. Socrates, Moses, Christ, Buddha, Mohammed, Martin Luther—all are illustrative of "great men" who have transcended, in substantial measure, existing social norms and more "deficient" codes of conduct.

Yet Durkheim's inclusion of the need for movers in history intimates, as an appendage, his own felt inner conflict in linking moral logic so intimately with social logic. Indeed, the "science of morality" he has been seeking may rest on a subtle form of reductionism. Durkheim's almost mimetic identification with the social world forces his conception of morality into problematic corners. In the words of one critic, "It precludes the legitimacy of a morality more adequate than systems of values and ideals of societies past, present and future."[18]

There is an even graver, more dangerous, implication in Durkheim's theory of moral development:

> For example, it implies that the authority, the norms and rules and principles that defined, for instance, the Nazi moral system must be considered as legitimate as any others that have served to sustain the social fabric of a collectivity.[19]

On the other hand, more sympathetic interpreters cite passages in Durkheim's work in which he contends that "all human societies are not of equal value."[20]

Despite these differences in interpretation, it must be granted that Durkheim's dominant sense of relativism tends to nullify the possibility of universalizing moral principles within his own paradigm. It is this departure from traditional post-Kantian ethics which has perhaps drawn the most obvious and sizable criticism from modern scholars and may be the primary reason for their relative lack of interest in Durkheim's model of moral development.

Nevertheless, Durkheim's paradigm can be disregarded only with peril because it does highlight social facts and actual social practices and contexts in a way which contemporary theories, from the psychoanalytic school to cognitive-structural psychology, sometimes seem to skim, gloss

---

[18]Prakash, Madhu Suri: Reflections on Durkheim's moral education. In Roemer, Robert E. (Ed.): *Philosophy of Education 1983: Proceedings of the Thirty-Ninth Annual Meeting of the Philosophy of Education Society.* Normal, Illinois State University, 1984, p. 344.

[19]*Ibid.* For more general treatments of Durkheim's analysis of moral development and education, see Lukes, Steven: *Emile Durkheim, His Life and Work: A Historical and Critical Study.* London, Allen Lane, 1973; Nisbet, Robert: *The Sociology of Emile Durkheim.* New York, Oxford U.P., 1974; and Gehlke, Charles E.: *Emile Durkheim's Contributions to Sociological Theory.* New York, AMS, 1968.

[20]Durkheim, Emile: *Moral Education,* p. 79.

over, or neglect altogether.[21] Durkheim was among the earliest researchers to make us aware of the critical importance of social forces and how they influence our interpretation of morality. Moreover, his sociology of knowledge reminds us that morality is a matter of concrete action and behavior as well as mere abstract thought, i.e., that what one *does* may be as significant as what one says.[22]

Finally, Durkheim makes us face an often overlooked question which may be crucial to moral accountability and moral development: given the powerful impingements of one's culture, how and to what extent can men be properly asked to perform in a "moral" manner? At what point are we really asking them to do what might be morally impossible?

Subsequent theorists to be dealt with in this text may or may not have paid heed to Durkheim's contributions. And that may help explain, at least in part, why we are still grappling with roughly the same central issues which he described so precisely nearly a century ago.

---

[21]In this connection, Durkheim's views dovetail with those of Freud to the extent that the competing demands of individual versus social life posit an inevitable, often irreconcilable, tension throughout human history. Some other contemporary theorists, such as Piaget and Kohlberg, have taken Durkheim very seriously, indeed. A substantial part of Piaget's *The Moral Judgment of the Child*, dealt with in Chapter 2 of this text, is devoted to a critical revision of Durkheim's theses in *Moral Education*. Meanwhile, Kohlberg has traced moral development theory according to "post-Durkheimian" and "post-Piagetian" paradigms in his "The development of children's orientation toward a moral order," *Vita Humana*, 6:11, 1963.

[22]For a broad view of the entire "attitude/behavior" dichotomy in social science research, see Deutscher, Irwin: *What We Say/What We Do.* Glenview, Scott, Foresman, 1973.

Chapter 2

MORAL DEVELOPMENT IN CHILDHOOD

FREUD: ENLIGHTENED SELF–INTEREST

PERHAPS the most significant, controversial theorist and therapist in the relatively short history of psychology, Sigmund Freud has enormously influenced personal and cultural judgments since he strode upon the intellectual scene in late-nineteenth century Austria. Theoretical constructions of personality, power, culture, child-rearing practices, even historical and literary criticism, to name only a few areas of discourse, were to be radically altered as a result. Freud's psychoanalytic contributions to the dialogue on morality are most germane to the developmental stages of early childhood—those years on which he laid so much stress. Indeed, his theory of morality, though more submerged, may be as important and controversial as his more widely known views of psychosexual development. Because of the magnitude of his impact, for good and/or ill, Freud's notions on morality will be analyzed as they apply to several major arenas of discussion and contention: (1) his overarching thesis of a "universal" paradigm which presumably governs all morality; (2) his specific treatment of alleged differences in how men and women develop; and (3) the ramifications and shortcomings of his theory for future constructions of moral reality.

As a "depth" psychologist who "pried open" the primacy of sexuality and the unconscious in a relatively closed Victorian world, Freud also carried on a battle similar to that waged by Durkheim in the sociological sphere. That is, Freud, like Durkheim, was interested principally in balancing the often irreconcilable demands of individual versus social life. Given his own theoretical constructs, Freud admits that the task of morality is ridden with unpleasant, almost impenetrable, conflict.

Though most students of psychology and education are doubtless familiar with Freud's tri-partite division of personality, i.e., the Id, Ego, and Superego, it may be helpful to explicate these theoretical constructs to show how they shed light on his theory of moral development.

16

Freud characterizes the *Id* as representative of animal-like instinctual impulses (largely of an unconscious sexual nature), the very core of human being and the repository for primary thought process. In essence, the Id signifies what we primordially desire to do if there were in fact no restrictions on our desires. These desires are most clearly demonstrable in dreams, fantasies, and similar unconscious thought phenomena. Freud further hypothesizes that the Id plays a predominant role in infancy and early childhood development, a period he considers most crucial in the overall development of the individual.

To counter-balance the Id, Freud introduces the term *Ego* to signify that self-regulating product of secondary (more conscious and rational) thought process which serves to bring the Id under some tenuous executory control. However, ego functions are refined only slowly and gradually, as the child grows and matures.

Most important for moral development in Freud's psychology is the role of the *Superego*, i.e., the inhibiting, restraining, prohibiting standards imposed on the child by outside social forces, initially and primarily by one's parents and later by teachers and other adult authority figures. From such parental and other external social sources, the child, if s/he is to be "normal" and "adjusted," develops an *ego-ideal* and *conscience*. Indeed, for Freud, guilt operating via the conscience is a form of "social glue" which cements, as it were, the cultural bonds of any society. Without guilt and conscience, life would degenerate into a "tooth-and-nail" existence and attendant societal chaos. Of course, according to Freud's psychic balancing scheme, excessive guilt disables individual action and may well lead to "neurotic," even "psychotic," behavior.

On the whole, however, Freud points to an optimal realization of self-control through an almost stoical exertion of rationality. He invokes such individual self-control because he contends that a substantial measure of repression is necessary to balance man's psychic apparatus, especially id impulses, with the demands of culture. Freud thus employs the concept of "repression" to regulate the seemingly irreconcilable conflict between individual autonomy and cultural restraint.

The term *repression* is used by Freud to express that most general, largely unconscious, defense mechanism which enables us to keep out of consciousness those thoughts, wishes, and desires too dangerous to one's conscious mental processes. A form of repression, *sublimation* refers to that defense mechanism which transforms id-like excitations into more socially acceptable patterns of behavior. Indeed, for Freud, sublimation serves to build culture in the form of art, religion, literature, etc. Accordingly, he calls upon man to sublimate what he assumes to be primary aggressive sex instincts with what is deemed necessary to constitute civilization:

> Civilization thus obtains mastery over the dangerous love of aggression in individuals by enfeebling and disarming it, and setting up an institution [superego] within their minds to keep watch over it, like a garrison in a conquered city.[1]

The demands of civilized life require man to struggle *with* repression, i.e., to practice a kind of frustrating, "heroic" individualism. To do otherwise would imperil cultural cohesion, which would, in turn, endanger individual man. This scenario summarizes Freud's version of "enlightened self-interest."

Even more significantly, this synopsis of Freud's psychology reveals how tenuous all morality is in Freud's eyes: it is a function of sublimations of the libido, i.e., those erotic, instinctual motive forces which presumably lay at the root of all human thinking and all human values. Freud traces such "higher" impulses largely to the superego in this very telling passage:

> It is easy to show that the ego ideal [of the superego] answers to everything that is expected of the higher nature of man. As a substitute for a longing for the father, it contains the germ from which all religions [and moral systems] have evolved. The self-judgment which declares that the ego falls short of its ideal produces the religious sense of humility to which the believer appeals in his longing. As a child grows up, the role of father is carried on by teachers and others in authority; their injunctions and prohibitions remain powerful in the ego ideal and continue, in the form of conscience, to exercise the moral censorship. The tension between the demands of conscience and the actual performances of the ego is experienced as a sense of guilt. Social feelings rest on identification with other people, on the basis of having the same ego-ideal.[2]

---

[1]Freud, Sigmund: *Civilization and Its Discontents,* J. Strachey (Tr.). New York, Norton, 1961, p. 105.

[2]Freud, Sigmund: The ego and the id. In J. Strachey (Ed.): *The Standard Edition of the Complete Psychological Works of Sigmund Freud.* London, Hogarth, vol. XIX, 1953–1966, p. 37. Presaging his pupil Jung's interest in unconscious "archetypes," Freud also relies on the power and urgency of the phylogenetic past: "The . . . tradition of the race and of the people, lives on in the ideologies of the super-ego, and yields only slowly to the influences of the present and to new changes . . ." Freud, Sigmund: New introductory lectures on psychoanalysis. *Ibid.,* vol. XXII, p. 67. This interest in the conservative phylogenetic past would also be carried on by G. Stanley Hall in America.

According to Seymour Fox, who has written a useful treatise on Freud's personality theory for education,[3] Freud's notions on moral development can be schematized in terms of how one's ego ideal organizes and interprets the so-called "higher" thought processes:

(1) religion = longing for father
(2) censorship and morality = sense of worthlessness
(3) submission to authority
(4) social feeling = identification with those with similar ego ideal

Given Freud's highly creative, but equally speculative, claims—most of which deal in *intrapsychic* phenomena seemingly immune to any inter-subjective public testing—one cannot help but inquire: From what sources does Freud's theory of morality originate in the first place? The response to that sobering question will hardly mollify more empirically-minded investigators. Resuscitating ancient mythology and Greek dramaturgy, Freud casts the foundation stones of morality in the parable of the "primal horde" and the tragedy of Oedipus and Electra. In the primal-horde parable, the sons of a clan commit patricide in order to replace the feared, dominating father figure. In terms of Oedipus and Electra, Freud hypothesizes that young boys fear castration and thus internalize and identify with father. In a certain sense, then, it is fear of castration which permits growth in morality in the male child's youthful development.

Feminist readers have long been suspicious of Freud's treatment of the Electra complex since it appears to place women in a much more precarious, problematic role. On Freud's terms, it becomes a psychological impossibility for girls to achieve a strong sense of morality because of what he assumes to be weaker superego development in females.[4] Unlike boys, who presumably fear castration and thus undergo value-internalization and value-identification through "castration anxiety," girls are already, as it were, "castrated" and cannot experience the same fears and threat of loss. As a consequence of this predicament, Freud postulates that young girls develop "penis envy," a very controversial notion which is still under severe attack by some less orthodox analysts, both feminist and nonfeminist.[5]

---

[3]Fox, Seymour: *Freud and Education*. Springfield, Thomas, 1975, p. 224.

[4]Freud, Sigmund: New introductory lectures on psychoanalysis. In *Standard Edition*, vol. XXII, p. 166.

[5]See the next section on Adler and Chapter 5 of this text, especially Carol Gilligan's counter-paradigm to the Freudian-Kohlbergian tradition in psychological theory.

For instance, Elizabeth Janeway's critical commentary on Freud's views echoes some of the reservations of later observers:

> Freud himself occasionally warned [in his essay on "Femininity"] . . . against the "superimposition" of unjustified significance on the facts of physical differences between the sexes. But these differences are just what he cites to account for the social roles of men and women, even though anyone reading him today can follow his arguments perfectly well (indeed better) by taking these differences as *symbolic* of assigned gender roles . . . of the socialization process of learning and accepting norms of behavior and expression.[6]

Adding further fuel to feminist criticism is the particular spotlight in which women are obliged to play their role in Freud's unfolding moral drama. Woman is viewed as the temptress and scorner of civilization, the Eve-like character who squanders men's attempts to sublimate their psychic energy, which is not limitless, into "higher" cultural tasks:

> The next discord is caused by women, who soon become antithetical to cultural trends, and spread around them their conservative influence—the women who at the beginning laid the foundation of culture by the appeal of their love. Women represent the interests of the family and the sexual life; the work of civilization has become more and more men's business; it confronts them with even harder tasks, compels them to sublimations of instinct which women are not easily able to achieve. Since man has not an unlimited amount of mental energy at his disposal, he must accomplish his tasks by distributing his libido to the best advantage. What he employs for cultural purposes he withdraws to a great extent from women and his sexual life.[7]

This lengthy quotation reveals several troublesome features in Freudian thought:

(1) its superimposition of an outmoded Newtonian (energy) model of physics onto psychic life;

(2) a bifurcation of the instincts and rationality in another classic Western formulation of "lower" and "higher" thought functions, assuming those functions can be so easily divided;

(3) a resultant positing of frustration for *both* men and women, the locus of that frustration resting on the roles assigned to the players; and

(4) Freud's almost imperceptible admission that those roles may be

---

[6]Janeway, Elizabeth: *Cross Sections: From a Decade of Change.* New York, Morrow, 1982, pp. 78–79. See also Freud: *Three Essays on the Theory of Sexuality* (1905), J. Strachey (Tr.). New York, Basic, 1962.

[7]Freud: *Civilization and Its Discontents*, p. 73.

more or less changeable, after all (i.e., his "Freudian slip" to the effect that "civilization *has become* more and more men's business").[8]

Freud's own student, Alfred Adler, would eventually come to the conclusion that Freud was unable to view the *social* context surrounding women's dilemma. Adler noted that dominant cultural groups and institutions, male or otherwise, are slow to remove blinders which bestow certain prerogatives of definitional power. He would also observe, with Georg Simmel, that other inhabitants of culture, seeking after solutions for social cohesion and personal solace, would mirror and accept such "authoritative" interpretations as if they were "universal" and "objective" guides to heart and mind for generations to come:

> The requirements of art, patriotism, morality in general and social ideals in particular, correctness in practical judgment and objectivity in theoretical knowledge, the energy and the profundity of life—all these are categories which belong as it were in their form and their claims to humanity in general, but in their actual historical configuration they are masculine throughout. Supposing that we describe these things, viewed as absolute ideas, by the single word "objective," we then find that in the history of our race the equation objective = masculine is a valid one.[9]

Thus, it became Adler's task to confront Freud's psychobiological model of morality. Subsequent theorists would come to regard Adler's critique as part of a "minority," or dissenting, view in academic psychology. Lately, this minority camp of psychologists and educators has begun to question what they term the fundamental "theoretical egocentrism" of Freudian and certain post-Freudian paradigms, including that of Kohlberg. For example, Robert Hogan argues that the dominant thrust of contemporary psychological theory has tended to wed Western thought to an "individualistic" perspective, thereby submerging such issues as "cooperation" and "social equality."[10] Such critics contend that these dominant models focus primarily on *internal, individual,* and *differential* measures of man and morality in their reliance on such constructs as "genetic

---

[8]For an incisive account of Freud's apparent inability to concede the full socio-historic underpinnings and implications of his own thought, see Marcuse, Herbert: *Eros and Civilization: A Philosophical Inquiry into Freud.* New York, Vintage, 1962.

[9]Simmel, Georg: *Philosophische Kultur,* as quoted in Horney, Karen: The flight from womanhood: The masculinity-complex in women as viewed by men and by women. In Kelman, H. (Ed.): *Feminine Psychology.* New York, Norton, 1967, pp. 55–56.

[10]Hogan, Robert: Theoretical egocentrism and the problem of compliance. *American Psychologist,* 30:533–540, 1975.

deficiencies," "weak superegos," and "pre/post/conventional personalities" (Kohlberg).[11] As a result of such theoretical constructions, a certain set of preconceptions about the nature of human beings, their morality, and the possibilities (or impossibilities) of socioeducational change begins to emerge. These formulations tend to "blame the victim," rather than the larger social order, for any obstacle or difficulty that the individual cannot overcome.

In the next section, we will look at Adler's often overlooked views on morality in an effort to clarify why and how he attempted to dislodge his master's theory and therapy. (Ironically, the relative neglect of Adler in academic psychology is also evident in Carol Gilligan's contemporary feminist paradigm of moral development. Gilligan never mentions Adler in her pioneering research although his theory, as will be shown, serves to foreshadow major themes in Gilligan's work.)

An appropriate place to conclude our study of Freud and to begin our elaboration of Adler is this candid confession of Freud—one which introduces us to Adler's serious misgivings about psychoanalytic theory and practice, particularly its characterization of "enlightened self-interest":

> In the years before the war, . . . I [Freud] made it a rule never to take for treatment anyone who was not *sui juis,* independent of others in all the essential relations of life.[12]

ADLER: SOCIAL INTEREST

Freud's original disciple, Adler, broke away from his teacher to form his own school ("Individual Psychology") on the ground that Freud's theory of sexuality was too reductionistic and that psychoanalytic dependence on "aggressive drives" posited an overly deterministic, largely intrapsychic and biological, view of human nature. In essence, Adler proposed to avoid any such reductionism and determinism by formulating a dialectical account of social dynamics and social relationships. Though Adler also emphasizes the importance of the early years of development, he is much more concerned with *social* influences which impinge

---

[11]William Ryan explores the enormous ramifications in public policy on social and moral issues generated by internal, intrapsychic paradigms in his *Blaming the Victim.* New York, Pantheon, 1976; and *Equality.* New York, Pantheon, 1981.

[12]Freud: *Introductory Lectures on Psycho-Analysis.* New York, Norton, 1929, pp. 385–386. Before World War I, sexual instincts were crucial in Freud's theory; thereafter, aggression and death instinct (Thanatos) seemed to become as critical. In either case, man was still viewed from an *internal* psychic lens, i.e., his motivations and determinant behavior appeared to lurk from *within* the individual.

upon thought, action, and behavior. Indeed, Adler's overarching theory of "social interest" places the whole range of viewing human behavior and morality in an entirely different perspective. Since Adler's major contributions have been somewhat submerged in the history of psychology and because his views of morality are unsystematic, it will be necessary to articulate those Adlerian concepts which seem particularly crucial to any exposition and assessment of his theory for moral development.

Adler claims that all humans enter the world in a position of "inferiority," i.e., we are all relatively helpless and dependent in infancy. From this original station in life, we gradually "strive toward overcoming" a feeling of powerlessness.[13] The conceptual vehicle by which Adler explains the progression from inferiority to "strivings for superiority" as one grows and matures has long been a prickly source of confusion, contention, and misconstruction among students in psychology. Adler borrowed Nietzsche's term "will to power" to describe how humans could "perfect" their existence, not to depict any yearnings for power and authority over other persons. In fact, on Adler's terms, any such egocentric striving would be viewed as "neurotic" and counter-productive to his own value system, which stressed "cooperation" as a prime motivating force, perhaps the most necessary human invention, in man's evolution. In some of his writings, Adler makes this point in clearer fashion:

> [The task of life is] to show the way in the reduction of the striving for personal power and in the education toward the community . . . and the development of social interest.[14]

In Adler's theory, then, "inferiority" and "power," properly defined, are integral to a fuller explanation of his most important principle, "social interest," which he characterizes as "compensation for all the natural weaknesses of individual human beings."[15] Social interest encompasses communal feeling, interpersonality, and empathy for others. According to Adler, the history of mankind is a movement toward more socially "superior," cooperative, and democratic directions necessitating equality in all aspects of life.[16] Indeed, he and his major disciple, Rudolf Dreikurs,

---

[13]Adler, Alfred: *Co-operation Between the Sexes: Writings on Women and Men, Love and Marriage, and Sexuality,* Ansbacher, Heinz L. and Rowena R. (Eds.). New York, Norton, 1978, pp. 49, 147–148, 168–169.

[14]Adler: *The Nervous Character: Fundamentals of a Comparative Individual Psychology and Psychotherapy,* 4th ed. Munich, Bergmann, 1928, pp. iv–vi.

[15]Adler: *Problems of Neurosis.* London, Kegan Paul, 1929, p. 31.

[16]Adler: *Social Interest: Challenge to Mankind* (1938). New York, Capricorn, 1964.

use the standard of "social interest" to judge the extent to which culture and individual personality have "matured":

> The degree of a person's social interest determines his ability and willingness to function socially; the lack of social interest is at the root of deficiencies, failures, and pathology. Thus, Adler found that social interest was a gauge for defining normalcy, both for the individual and for the group.[17]

Adlerians conceive of social interest as both inborn and capable of nurture and development as the child grows and matures. Accordingly, children should be given social tasks and responsibilities to perform, depending on their level of maturity. Household chores, family helping, and school duties, as examples, breed those patterns of behavior which eventually instill habits of both interdependence and independence in children. Paralleling Freud's concern for "reality testing" through ego strengthening, Adlerians admonish against "pampering," a practice they regard as injurious as child abuse or neglect.[18] For instance, an isolate, self-centered "princely" child bears little mark of that indelible imprint of social interest which Adlerians insist is required for the continuous growth of mankind as a whole and for that person as a self-sustaining individual:

> The very concept of "human being" includes our entire understanding of social feeling. . . . [We have] always lived in groups, unless separated from one another artificially or through insanity. . . . In the deepest sense, the feeling for the logic of human living together is social feeling . . . [19]

With specific reference to early development, Dreikurs notes that "the child, at any age level, is a typical human being who wants his place in the group and rebels against being subdued."[20] Taking up Adler's work, Dreikurs extends the notion of "social interest" to include "social equality" and democratic alignments among all persons, regardless of their station in life. Indeed, he describes egalitarian relationships as the "only stable basis for [any] social relationships."[21]

However, the apparent thrust of Adlerian arguments for democratic cooperation as an approximate ideal of human behavior is not meant to

---

[17]Dreikurs, Rudolf: *Social Equality: The Challenge of Today.* Chicago, Regnery, 1971, p. viii.

[18]Dreikurs and Soltz, Vicki: *Children: The Challenge.* New York, Hawthorn, 1964. This interest in "reality testing" is also reflected in the work of Freud's other pupil, C.G. Jung.

[19]Adler: *Co-operation Between the Sexes,* p. 107.

[20]Dreikurs: *Social Equality,* p. 80.

[21]*Ibid.,* p. 115.

discount adult guidance of the child. Though Adlerians stress the importance of generating egalitarian conditions, they grant the necessity of significant adult presence in assuring the evolution of a discernible, not chaotic, social order. For that matter, they insist that "learning respect for order" is essential for establishing stability and rationality in the child's surroundings.[22] (In this sense, Adlerians seem not too far removed from Durkheim's traditional adult role model of moral development. The Adlerian reliance on adult authority also underlines a critical difference in its theory and practice as opposed to that of Piaget, who argues that peer interaction can substitute effectively for such adult supervision. Research for and against Piaget's position is discussed subsequently.) Evidently, Adlerians, like many parents, have noticed that even young children have been known to "read" and manipulate their elders. Consequently, a primary task of Adlerian family therapy becomes that of assisting parents and teachers in locating and rechanneling children's "faulty" motivations (and "mistaken behavior") in more "socially useful" directions.

Dreikurs attempts to balance the extremes of "authoritarian" and "permissive" child rearing through the use of the learning device, "natural and logical consequences":

> What would be the natural consequences of forgetting one's lunch? One would go hungry . . . This is the natural consequence of her forgetfulness.[23]

> Consequences, which must be natural and logical to the disturbances of order, are self-evident . . . it is order and reality . . . not the arbitrary power of adults, which brings about the unpleasant consequences.[24]

Some critics have characterized this Adlerian teaching tool as "an interesting deployment of 'intentions' and 'consequences' " but one which tends, in reality, to subordinate the autonomy of the learner to parental and environmental influence, i.e., a measure which parallels behavioral forms of child rearing.[25]

Yet the Adlerian interest in addressing subordinate/superordinate relationships does generate promise for growth in democratic and social

---

[22]Dreikurs and Soltz: *Children: The Challenge,* pp. 96–102.

[23]*Ibid.,* p. 76.

[24]Dreikurs: The cultural implications of reward and punishment. *International Journal of Social Psychiatry,* 4:177, 1948.

[25]DeVitis, Joseph L.: Cooperation and social equality in childhood: Adlerian and Piagetian lessons. *Journal of Research and Development in Education,* 17:23, 1984.

morality, particularly in the case of the sexes. For Adler, unequal sexual relationships constituted a bone of contention, an unwritten "power struggle," as it were, for both sexes. Accordingly, he advocated the "equal worth of the sexes":

> Women have to suffer because in our culture it is much easier for a man to play the leading role. But the man also suffers because by this fictitious [spurious] superiority he loses touch with the underlying values.[26]

Adler coined the term *masculine protest* to express the feeling which either sex experiences in contexts involving inferior/superior social interactions and distinctions. Another widely misunderstood Adlerian concept, *masculine protest* implied a present, but changeable, condition of "feminine" traits, principally a feeling of inferiority as a result of given, not necessary, social conditions of male domination. Adler envisioned an evolving antithesis to this condition in the form of "strivings for superiority" which would be refined and perfected to the point of overcoming subordinate or oppressive circumstances.[27]

Thus Adler viewed "masculine protest" as a culturally-biased criterion favorable to males, and not on the basis of physiological sex differentiation. His standard implied that sexual distinctions were largely the result of unnecessary *social* determinations, not biological necessities. In this connection, it is interesting to speculate upon that intriguing distinction made by one of Freud's major recent revisionists, Herbert Marcuse. The latter uses the concepts "basic" versus "surplus" repression to clarify those kinds of repressive measures which are necessary and unnecessary. "Basic" repression refers to that modification of the "instincts necessary for the perpetuation of the human race in civilization," e.g., provision of food and shelter and combatting of disease. "Surplus" repression refers to those additive "restrictions necessitated by social domination," i.e., layered forms of constraint over and above that which is essential to the maintenance of civilized life. According to Marcuse, surplus-repression has been caused by socio-historic conditions, which are amenable to social change.[28] The point to be made in the Freud/Adler dispute is that

---

[26]Adler: *The Education of Children.* New York, Greenberg, 1930, p. 222.

[27]Ansbacher: In Adler, *Co-operation Between the Sexes,* pp. 155–156, 162–164. Freud castigated Adler's notion of "masculine protest," couching it as a veiled reflection and consequent deflection of "universal castration anxiety" and common aggressive propensities. See Freud: Analysis terminable and interminable. In Strachey, James (Ed.): *The Collected Papers of Sigmund Freud.* New York, Basic, 1950, vol. V, p. 357n.

[28]Marcuse: *Eros and Civilization,* pp. 32–34.

Adler seems to have recognized Marcuse's distinctions in ways which Freud did not:

> In our society, an exaggerated importance is attached to masculinity, and the inferiority of the female sex is assumed as a generally established principle. Even if sexual equality is admitted theoretically, [social] actions ... usually speak the contrary. . . . From the earliest days the child is led to believe that the male is the more valuable sex.[29]

Consequently, Adler attempted to reduce the strife and competition attending these unequal and oppressive social conditions. Unlike Freud, who was very dubious of social change, Adler participated in social reform. For example, he organized child guidance clinics and experimental schools throughout Austria.[30]

This curious development allows us to find clues to such conclusions in the manner in which Freud and Adler conceived of (1) their own therapeutic practice and (2) their analysis of the role and scope of the family and other social institutions. Whereas Freudian therapy emphasizes the primacy of the analyst as a distant, but authoritative, figure, Adlerians stress the import of fostering social interest via the client's own "expert" private logic and intentions. And whereas self-insight is a sufficient end in psychoanalytic psychiatry, it is usually insufficient, sometimes unnecessary, in Individual Psychology.

The goal of Adlerian counseling is to move the client into the *social* arena since most seemingly psychological problems are viewed, by Adlerians, as primarily *social* problems. Freud's predominantly internal, intrapsychic perspective fails to grasp this point fully. For Adlerians, change in behavior is an essential clue to any growth in self-insight, i.e., basing one's judgment solely on "thoughts, desires, and emotions [fails] to give sufficient ... consideration [to] our actions—to what we *do*.[31] Indeed, some therapists have argued that excessive self-analysis could conceivably ignite a flight into various forms of pathology (e.g., narcissism and paranoia).[32]

Other critics have leveled a more basic attack on the manner in which psychoanalysts conceptualize all human relations, particularly family

---

[29]Way, Lewis: *Adler's Place in Psychology: An Exposition of Individual Psychology.* New York, Collier, 1962, p. 34.

[30]Dreikurs: Early experiments in social psychiatry. *International Journal of Social Psychiatry,* 7:141–147, 1961; Papanek, Ernst: *The Austrian School Reform.* New York, Fell, 1962; and DeVitis, Joseph L.: Freud, Adler, and women: powers of the "weak" and "strong," *Educational Theory,* in press.

[31]Dreikurs: On knowing oneself. *International Journal of Individual Psychology,* 3:13–23, 1937.

[32]Laing, R.D.: *The Divided Self.* New York, Pantheon, 1969.

structures. These observers make the case that psychoanalysis tends to reduce human relations to the level and pattern of the psyche within the substructure of the nuclear family. In their view, Freud tended to collapse all social action so as to picture it as a recapitulation of emotional sets within the mental frame of the family. As such, according to this critique, Freud erroneously universalizes certain internalized family matrices, thus disabling him from weighing—or even seeing—the impact of overarching, perhaps more dominant, external social structures of particular times and places (in his case, patriarchal Victorian society):

> The hero [Freudian man] is able to attain to "individual psychology" only because he internalizes his father at a deep enough level; he creates an "ego-ideal" in himself. Hence the mechanism for reproducing individuals—those who are free, who can think, who can restrain their emotions, who can be distinctive—is the key to history ... [and] the mechanism for this degree of individualization is the patriarchal nuclear family.[33]

Cultural and literary critics have depicted Freud's characterization of morality as "enlightened self-interest" in more comical, but deadly serious and tragic, overtones:

> The aim of Freudian psychiatry is ... the reconciliation of instinct and intelligence. The intellect is set to helping the instincts develop, tolerantly, like a prudent teacher. Conscience, however, directs us to repress the instincts. The conscience-stricken thus do not appear by Freudian standards to be very intelligent. By viewing conscience as in opposition to intelligence, Freud exhibits a prejudice against virtue fairly common among secular intellectuals—the idea that the merely good person is not likely to be either very clever or very strong.[34]

> [In] the suppression of an overactive conscience by the rest of the mind ... the leader most prompt to appear ... [is] Enlightened Self-Interest ... It is essentially the black and white Jolly Roger, with these words written beneath the skull and crossbar, "The hell with you, Jack, I've got mine!" [Thus] ... a normal person, functioning well on the upper levels of a prosperous, industrialized society, can hardly hear his conscience at all.[35]

Given this doleful state of affairs, Vonnegut, the novelist, can locate only a rare few individuals, usually branded as "fools" by the larger

---

[33]Poster, Mark: *Critical Theory of the Family.* New York, Seabury, 1980, pp. 34–35. Cf. Freud: *Group Psychology and the Analysis of the Ego,* J. Strachey (Tr.). New York, Norton, 1965.

[34]Rieff, Philip: *Freud: The Mind of the Moralist.* Garden City, Doubleday, 1959, pp. 305–306.

[35]Vonnegut, Kurt, Jr.: *God Bless You, Mr. Rosewater: Or Pearls Before Swine.* New York, Dell, 1965, pp. 42–43.

society, "who reach biological maturity still loving and wanting to help their fellow men."[36]

The essential point of this cultural and literary excursion has been to show the strain of morality which is apparently missing in Freudian theory and therapy and to exemplify how Adler presages present moral paradigms which consider the primacy of "sympathy, compassion, and human concern."[37] It is in this light that Adler can be seen rightly as a forerunner to some of the kernel ideas in Gilligan's current feminist model of moral development—one which supports a moral language of care, responsibility, and not wanting to hurt others.[38] Indeed, a reacquaintance with Adler might actually serve to extend Gilligan's thesis in that the latter tends to speak solely of *private* social relationships (e.g., family members, friends, and colleagues) rather than a larger social community.[39]

Thus Adler's theory highlights other possible perspectives, e.g., those of *collective* and *external* reference, which certain critics claim have been submerged in the history of psychology.[40] In David Bakan's more recent terminology, Adler points to possibilities for *communal* as well as merely "agentic" (self/power) development.[41]

All this is not meant to convey the impression that Adler was theorizing without moral or social blinders. Throughout much of his writing, Adler appears to be unaware that he is committing the naturalistic fallacy in argumentation by mixing claims for "is" and "ought." In many ways, his theory is couched in prescriptive terms which he would like to maintain are purely descriptive:

> Individual Psychology ... regards as "right" that which is useful for the community. ... Every departure from the social standard is an offense against right and brings with it a conflict with the objective laws and objective necessi-

---

[36]*Ibid.*

[37]Blum, Lawrence A.: *Friendship, Altruism and Morality.* London, Routledge and Kegan Paul, 1980.

[38]Gilligan, Carol: *In A Different Voice: Psychological Theory and Women's Development.* Cambridge: Harvard U.P., 1982.

[39]Sichel, Betty A.: Moral development and education: men's language of rights and women's language of responsibility. *Contemporary Education Review,* 2:33–42, 1983.

[40]In his *Equality,* Ryan elucidates these individual/internal versus collective/external distinctions in clear, common-sense fashion. Freud took collective action to be largely "regressive" and antithetical to intelligent self-restraint. See Poster: *Critical Theory of the Family,* pp. 37–38.

[41]Bakan, David: *The Duality of Human Existence.* Chicago, Rand McNally, 1966. See also Sampson, Edward E.: Psychology and the American ideal. *Journal of Personality and Social Psychology,* 35:767–782, 1977.

ties of reality. . . . [It] violates an immanent social ideal which everyone of us, consciously or unconsciously, carries in himself.[42]

In addition, Adler's social analysis is lacking in rigor, depth, and precision. That is to say, his account of interpersonal social relationships does not elaborate fully the larger, more amorphous, power structures and sociopolitical constraints which more recent critics have observed.[43] Nor does he entirely fathom the deep-seated imponderables which might make for well-nigh irreconcilable conflict, as Freud himself recognized so well. As an example, Adler fails to distinguish adequately the boundaries between social "cooperation" and social "constraint" or "conformity."[44]

At base, both Freud and Adler are relying upon theoretical constructs— be they "aggressive instincts" (Freud) or "cooperation" (Adler)—which have not been conclusively warranted in either clinical or experimental studies. Perforce it is extremely difficult to prove that propensities of any sort are "built into" human nature—a monumental point of controversy at least since John Locke introduced his notion of "tabula rasa" (blank slate) in the 17th century and radically challenged classical conceptions of man's "goodness" or "evil." (Of course, future theorists and practitioners—from Carl Rogers to sociobiologists—would continue to make such assumptions about the nature of man, however far apart their differentiations and distinctions on such matters as "altruism" and "aggression" might take them.)[45]

JUNG: FROM FANTASY TO REALITY

Carl Jung, another of Freud's original disciples and apostates, does not formulate a systematic account of the contours and nuances of moral development. Indeed, moral growth is assumed by Jung to be a lifelong process which results in "self-actualization" for relatively few individuals only by the time they reach middle age or beyond. Nevertheless, Jung's insights into child maturation will be focused on in this section for the richness of sources he brings to bear on wide ranging issues and because of the imaginative, if not always convincing, way in which he views the

---

[42]Adler: *The Education of Children*, p. 21.

[43]Jacoby, Russell: *Social Amnesia: A Critique of Contemporary Psychology from Adler to Laing.* Boston, Beacon, 1976.

[44]DeVitis: Cooperation and social equality in childhood: Adlerian and Piagetian lessons, p. 24.

[45]See, for example, Rogers, Carl R.: *On Becoming a Person.* Boston, Houghton Mifflin, 1961; and Wilson, Edward O.: *On Human Nature.* New York, Bantam, 1979.

child's inner struggle to come to grips with collectivity and individuality. Once again, we are dealing with a psychological theorist who is bent on synthesizing the elements of stability and autonomy.

Jung's intense interest in archaeology, anthropology, and religion led him to study primitive artifacts from various cultures which seemed to have traits in common, e.g., the adoration of the Virgin, or Mother, figure as well as universal curiosities attached to the Circle (Mandala). From such exploration, Jung concluded that human forces derive primordially from a collective base and that all men share certain core components from that human condition. At root, this primitive collective sharing rests in the unconscious. The task of moral development is to differentiate those components of the unconscious which will make for a balanced psychic life, to eventually enable the conscious personality to become self-regulating and unified in all its parts.[46] In psychodynamic terms, Jung's neo-analytic mission is that of permitting the relatively impersonal collective unconscious to be refined to the point that it is appropriated by one's personal ego.

For the child, this development follows along the lines of a very gradual shifting from fantasy to reality; and this unfolding is ascertained by one's ability to distinguish those two realms:

> Development starts from a condition of complete participation in, and undifferentiation from, the inner [fantasy] and outer [real] world in which it lives; it then proceeds by way of the development of its ego, and the separation of its personality from its anonymous identity with all existing facts. That is why the word "I" only enters the consciousness of the child comparatively late, towards the end of the third year of life; a sign that it is only then that the first appreciable and conscious traces of an ego-personality as opposed to the collective psyche appears.[47]

The most primitive traces of the developing psyche, for Jung, are located in what he terms the "archetypes," symbolic representations of those instinctual clusters of ideas which have been formed unconsciously over the centuries. They are part of one's personal as well as collective unconscious and allow the child to draw, as it were, "self-portraits" of

---

[46]Notice should be taken of Jung's similarities with Freud and Durkheim. With Freud, Jung emphasizes the primacy of the unconscious, though his use of anthropological evidence leads him to develop a separate category for the *collective* unconscious—to some critics, an illustration of highly mystical constructs which have been a principal source of reaction against Jung. With Durkheim (though he never mentions him), Jung is attempting to integrate the competing interests of the collective and the individual into an ongoing "self-regulating" system.

[47]Adler, Gerhard: *Studies in Analytical Psychology.* New York: Putnam, 1967, p. 127.

his/her instincts so that s/he can imagine and perfect his idea of certain mental constructs, e.g., "mother," "father," and the like.[48] Jolan Jacobi, still perhaps the most lucid interpreter of Jung's psychology, gives this illustration of the role and scope of archetypes:

> For example, the archetype "Mother" is ... pre-existent and superordinate to every form of manifestation of the "motherly." It is a constant core of meaning, which can take on all the aspects and symbols of the "motherly." The primordial image of the mother and the characteristics of the "Great Mother" with all her paradoxical traits are the same in the soul of present-day man as in mythological times.... Realizing or becoming conscious means ... forming a world by drawing distinctions [among such traits and characteristics].[49]

Thus, according to Jung, the maturation process becomes one of restructuring and integrating fantasy life to make it complementary with "real" life through an ongoing broadening of consciousness. The child must inevitably separate himself from the "land of childhood" (fantasy) by employing reason, melding it to his earlier "historical soul" (archetypes) and largely instinctual existence. At the same time, throughout life, the compensating features of instinct and reason, fantasy and reality, must be assimilated constantly if man is to live a whole, unified life. That is to say, the instinctual resources of childhood ideally provide a perennial flow of life force; without them, mature man takes on a "dried up," sterile, overly rationalized visage.[50] After all, it is fantasy which breeds creativity and sensitive reflection.

This picture of the slowly unfolding personality allows us to see how Jung visualizes the manner in which divergent kinds of thinking, apparently so crucial in moral reasoning, develop. Even by way of the primitive archetypes, the child is beginning to experience, in some respects, how others before him have acted and judged life. In this fashion, s/he will gradually learn to discern similarities and differences in humanity, i.e., how and why men have lived collectively and individ-

---

[48]Classical scholars will note Jung's borrowing of this conception from St. Augustine's notion of "reminiscence," an idea later re-translated by Plato to mean "primordial image," or the "essence" of reality. Jung's treatment of archetypes also places him in the psychological tradition which insists that ontogeny (the single individual organism) recapitulates phylogeny (the group, species, or race)—a very debatable theory made more explicit in G. Stanley Hall's studies of adolescence.

[49]Jacobi, Jolan: *The Psychology of Jung,* K.W. Bash (Tr.). New Haven: Yale U.P., 1943, pp. 44–45.

[50]In this regard, Jung is critical of the Western penchant to "over-differentiate" consciousness. He was more hopeful that Oriental culture would offer a more compensating balance between the conscious and the unconscious, as in the practice of meditation. See Jung: *The Integration of the Personality,* S.M. Dell (Tr.). London: Kegan Paul, 1940, p. 106.

ually. Through such learning, later critical distinctions can be made—distinctions which may eventuate in a psychic life of freedom from the crowd and an integrated view of how cooperative social life can also be morally beneficial.

To recap Jung's theory, let us return to the specifics of his developmental model. Though the first few years of life are as significant to Jung as they are to his master Freud, Jung likewise insists that there is little conscious development during those years (thus his rationale for minimizing the use of psychotherapy with young children). The child remains largely unconscious to himself from ages 1–3; during which time s/he exhibits many manifestations of an animal creature.[51] "Only when the child begins to say "I" [at approximately 3–5 years of age] is there any perceptible continuity of consciousness."[52] In effect, s/he is developing consciousness of his/her ego. It is generally at puberty that youth grow in the direction of independence.

During childhood the role of the school can be vital in refining and taming instincts, differentiating youth from their more "primitive" impulses, i.e., making them more compatible with civilized existence. In this regard, Jung seems to be implicitly echoing much of Durkheim's argument for the necessity of socialization. Like Durkheim, he emphasizes that the teacher influences mainly as a role model by the force of his/her personality. The teacher also serves to wean the child from overdependence on his/her parents and the immediate environment.

What kind of educational development would Jung recommend? His response is consistent with his general theory of the "integrated personality." Jung believes firmly in the importance of a broad liberal education, one in which the humanities are the central activity and content of the curriculum. He warns roundly against overspecialization and a disregard for the mistakes of the past. In short, Jung is committed to a developmental education in which past roots can be gradually and naturally embedded in the child's present and future life, ideally allowing him/her a total integration of the unconscious and conscious, the world of fantasy melding into the experience of reality.[53]

---

[51]Once again, Jung intimates, along with G.S. Hall, that individuals evolve through the same stages, from "primitive" to "progressive" forms, as their species. Jung's "animal" characterization is also remindful of Piaget's description of the predominantly "egocentric" traits of early childhood.

[52]Jung: The development of personality: papers on child psychology, education, and related subjects. In R.F.C. Hull (Tr.): *Collected Papers of C.G. Jung.* New York, Pantheon, 1954, vol. 17, p. 52.

[53]*Ibid.*, pp. 144–145. Of course, some critics have challenged Jung's allegiance to "past roots" on the

Specifically, Jung divides the developmental span of education into three parts: (1) education through example; (2) collective education; and (3) individual education. These roughly parallel the progression from unconscious education to more individuated, consciously differentiated, education as the person matures and balances his/her own personality.

By "education through example," Jung concerns himself with those early stages of child development when the young person is "more or less identical with its environment, and especially with its parents," that period in which s/he is still struggling to mold his/her primitive, largely unconscious, psyche. Though this mode of development ultimately gives way to collective and individual education, Jung is insistent on the primacy of "contagion through experience" in building psychic identity throughout his pedagogic agenda.[54]

Jung's translation of "collective" education is not to be confused with mass schooling. Instead it refers to adherence to certain general rules, principles, and methodologies in order to establish a modicum of uniformity in the culture. However, Jung's version of socialization does not call for a "lock-step" form of uniformity which would crush unique individuality. As such, Jung is concerned that personhood be protected in the security of individual judgments—many of which may not have recourse to rules and regulations. In this, he seems to be searching, albeit unsystematically and willy-nilly, for those same kinds of safeguards on autonomy which interested and confounded Durkheim. Unfortunately, Jung likewise makes no concrete recommendations for such securities on self-determination.[55]

As the pupil grows and matures, "individual" education takes on more and more relevance. It involves a subordination of the levelling devices, codes, and rules of conduct maintained in collective education. The clue to whom shall attain toward individual education is to be found in those students—those "gifted" individuals—who have shown resistance to collective education. On the one hand, such students may exhibit "defects" —mental, physical, or psychological. On the other hand, giftedness may

---

ground that such a notion may have influenced his flirtation with Nazism. This issue may be part and parcel of the same socialization question which was seen to plague Durkheim earlier.

[54]Jung: The significance of the unconscious in individual education. In R.F.C. Hull (Tr.): *Collected Papers of C.G. Jung,* vol. 17, pp. 149–150. The overarching factor of introjection of experience is also seen in Erik Erikson's concept of "identity crisis" discussed in Chapter Three of this text.

[55]*Ibid.*

entail some special attitude or ability, i.e., what is commonly referred to today as the "exceptional" child or person. According to Jung, such "specialness" is usually derived from the teachings, or lack thereof, in one's home environment.[56]

Thus, Jung's little-known views on education are intriguing for a number of reasons. First, though his theory is very speculative and impressionistic, it concurs to a remarkable degree with some more descriptive findings in the current literature of moral development. These findings, e.g., those of Kohlberg to be discussed in Chapter 5, suggest that the large majority of human beings may not achieve a very high level of morality throughout their lives. Conversely, only a small minority seems to be able to reach beyond "conventional" modes of moral thinking. Second, Jung's speculations have even more serious implications in terms of attempting to decide when, how, and why "individual idiosyncracies" must be blunted or denied expression. Of course, this issue also carries with it the companion problem of deciding *whose* idiosyncratic thought and action should be stifled and who, indeed, should be the judges in that process of determination. In a curious way, then, the highly individualistic thought of Jung might lead to another form of behavioral engineering—or even to practices beyond the pale of controlled manipulation of human behavior.

Such dire warning signals are implicit in some of Jung's more widely known concepts, which will now be scrutinized in light of his so-called "typological" theory. Throughout his own life, Jung employed the Circle symbol to represent the totality of psychic life in its basic functional components: thinking, feeling, intuition, and sensation. The first two functions, thinking and feeling, are evaluative in that they make use, respectively, of cognitive and affective judgment from the standpoint of "true-false" and "agreeable-disagreeable" discernments. The second pair of functions, intuition and sensation, are termed "irrational" by Jung because they involve simply perceptual phenomena which are irreducible to cogitative interpretation. According to Jung, each and every person predominates in certain of these functions. It is such predominance which marks the general orientation of one's personality. Regrettably, Jung gives no clear or real reasons for his typological designations

---

[56]*Ibid.*, p. 151.

beyond stating that he can "only point to the fact that this conception has shaped itself out of many years' experience."[57]

The development of psychological attitudes is related to several concepts with which Jung's name is even more widely popular: "extroversion" and "introversion." For Jung, these distinctive psychic orientations condition one's entire behavioral tone in all its manifestations. An extravert "thinks, feels, and acts in reference to . . . [external] objects."[58] That is, s/he is primarily influenced by consensual, collectively validated, social norms and codes of conduct. On the other hand, introverts relate negatively to external objects, instead relying on their own subjective experience. Consonant with his interest in balancing opposites in order to form a more total personality. Jung claims that the unconscious of each type carries on the psychic work left undone by one's consciousness. In other words, the unconscious of the extrovert is introverted, and vice-versa for the introvert.

Lurking beneath the surface of Jung's attempt at dialectical synthesis is, then, the crag-like possibility that man is fighting an uphill battle against dualisms throughout development. This cruel, harsh reality is perhaps best demonstrated in Jung's notion of the "shadow." This archetypal figure expresses the symbolic "other aspect," or "darkness," which is inseparable from totality. For Jung, the point of evil is to elucidate that which is goodness and light, to permit us more perceptive penetration into moral enlightenment.[59] However, the shadow concept poses greater, well-nigh insurmountable, imponderables to the extent that, if Jung is correct, evil may indeed be an irreducible fact of human existence, not to be overcome lightly.[60]

To conclude our inquiry into Jung's neo-analytic contributions on a

---

[57]Jung: *Psychological Types — Or The Psychology of Individuation*, H.G. Baynes (Tr.). London, Kegan Paul, 1923, p. 547. Jung's lack of reasons for his typology has not curtailed efforts to use it in modern psychological practice, particularly in career and vocational assessment; e.g., the Myers-Briggs inventory is based largely on Jung's speculations.

[58]Jung: *Modern Man in Search of a Soul*, C.F. Baynes (Tr.). London, Kegan Paul, 1933, p. 99.

[59]Jung: *Two Essays on Analytical Psychology*, H.G. & C.F. Baynes (Tr.). London, Bailliere, 1928, p. 266. Jung's play on opposites which constantly merge is also seen in his concepts, "anima" and "animus" (male/female "soul images," or archetypes). Such dualisms have not sat well with some feminists, despite Jung's protestations that he has learned much from his patients (mostly female). See his: *Memories, Dreams, Reflections.* New York, Pantheon, 1973.

[60]See Jung: *Letters*, vol. II, R.F.C. Hull (Tr.). Princeton: Princeton U.P., 1975, p. 624: "I am strongly convinced that the evil principle prevailing in this world leads the unrecognized spiritual need into perdition, if it is not counteracted either by real religious insight or the protective wall of human community."

higher note, Jung does challenge us to face the critical aim of perhaps all moral life: how to emerge as an individual while maintaining harmony with the totality of life surrounding one's existence. He divides this monumental task into stages of childhood and adulthood in such a way that the first stage elicits knowledge of the boundaries of individuality while reserving the second stage for a more integrated understanding of how man places himself in the vastness of the Universe:

> The first half of life is spent mainly in finding out who we are, through seeing ourselves in our interaction with others . . . the realization of what we can do by ourselves, what we can do with the help of others, and what we cannot do at all. The mature [person] has discovered himself or herself as a differentiated personality spending his days and nights doing what he is fitted for by his own nature, without frittering away his energies in pointless strivings or useless regrets.[61]

The constant upshot of Jung's recommendations for child rearing is his insistence that the young person be exposed carefully and gradually to life's realities, both its good and evil sides. Too precipitate over-exposure disarms the child, leaving him unprotected and defenseless. At the same time, his/her fantasy world has already been inhabited by ghosts and goblins—precursors of the unsafe later life that will have to be faced and dealt with in head-on fashion.[62]

Accordingly, we might summarize the implications of Jung's thought for moral development in the following manner: (1) man should be treated as an unfolding individual, slowly and relentlessly differentiating himself from the mass of humanity; (2) "every stage of life has its specific duty, and he who does not fulfill these specific duties, that is who does not live through that particular phase, has failed to experience one aspect of life, and the price of this refusal is either stultification and

---

[61]Singer, June: *Boundaries of the Soul: The Practice of Jung's Psychology.* New York, Doubleday Anchor, 1973, pp. 277–278. Put in another way, "The first half of life is mainly dominated by the task of adaptation to the external world, implying an unfolding and expansion. In the second half of life, we are confronted with the need to discover the *meaning* of our life in particular and of life in general." Adler, Gerhard: *Studies in Analytical Psychology,* p. 138.

[62]For example, the child's learning to overcome the fear of death permits him/her to be better prepared for future lessons in life. See Adler, Gerhard: *Studies in Analytical Psychology,* p. 133: "He who tries to escape life, that is the development of his own individual personality, falls a victim to life. Only he who accepts life with all its complications and conflicts attains to full living consciousness, enabling him to find a new life-centre beyond the reach of present entanglements. Only by a full experience of life can we become conscious." In this same vein, Jung's teachings strikingly resemble those of Alfred Adler. The latter also cautions against "pampering" or "spoiling" the child on the ground that it fosters little courage in his/her struggle with reality.

numbness or a neurosis";[63] and (3) man should be allowed to synthesize life in order for it to take on more holistic meaning. Thus, strong elements of stoicism, integration, and transcendence underlie Jung's psychology. They bespeak the fact that moral life is something that is expected as a natural eventuality, but one which is exceedingly difficult in its execution. In the long run, Jungian man has not only "enlightened self-interest" in morality (Freud's view), but also an obligation to the human species. This almost religious attitude forms a synthesis between oneself and the rest of human, natural, and divine existence, as in the "great penetration" of Lao-Tse. And because this task of life is so great, very few persons approach "self-actualization," i.e., the creation of a whole personality wherein one's self becomes fully defensible and indestructible.[64]

BANDURA: SOCIAL LEARNING THEORY

Although this approach was initially sketched by Miller and Dollard,[65] Albert Bandura rightfully receives the credit for developing social learning theory. The theory emphasizes social situations as the context in which behavior is learned. The mediation of other people is a critical requirement for needs satisfaction. Bandura holds that behavior changes that occur through classical and operant conditioning are mediated by processes of cognition and social regulation.[66]

Bandura, while recognizing that learning can occur through direct experience, emphasizes that learning can take place by observing the behavior of others. These social responses are referred to as modeling or observational learning. A child who observes a person (model) perform an act is more likely to behave in a similar manner. Repeated trials may be unnecessary; the child can learn the behavior merely through observation. Children learn social behaviors by observing significant

---

[63]*Ibid.*

[64]Jung describes his idealized "self-actualized" person as one who is "excellent in knowledge" and "excellent in will," but who is "no arrogant superman." Jung: *Two Essays on Analytical Psychology,* p. 264. Nevertheless, such characterizations have not quelled the tide of criticism against Jung's evident elitist tendencies and his apparent lack of sympathy for the oppressed and persecuted who inhabit the human race. For instance, documentation of Jung's anti-Semitic leanings appears in Karier, Clarence J.: The ethics of a therapeutic man: C.G. Jung. *Psychoanalytic Review,* 63:1, 1976, 115–146.

[65]Miller, N.E. and Dollard, J.: *Social Learning and Imitation.* New Haven: Yale University Press, 1941.

[66]Bandura, Albert: *Social Learning Theory.* New York: Prentice-Hall, 1977.

people in their lives. These observations are stored as mental images and symbolic representations that help them model behavior.

Bandura rejected the unidirectional behavioristic, stimulus-response view of the effects of environment on the individual. Instead his theme is reciprocal determinism, a process by which personal factors, environmental factors, and behavior operate as interlocking determinants of one another. For example, aggressive children expect other children to act hostilely toward them and this causes the aggressive child to act aggressively. Thus they create through their actions a hostile environment while children with friendly modes of response generate an amicable social situation.[67]

The child needs to be attentive to what the model does, admire the model, and have the capability of performing the modeled act. Other than parents, the model the child is most likely to emulate is one who can provide rewards, control the consequences of behavior, and who possesses high status. Modeling fosters learning of different kinds of behavior such as play patterns, aggression, language, and many social behaviors. Modeling may also create such undesirable responses as overaggressiveness, dishonesty, and deceitfulness.

Bandura and Walters compared 26 highly aggressive adolescent boys and 26 control boys.[68] The aggressive boys were under the supervision of probationary services and had a history of aggressive behavior, whereas the control group was identified by school counselors as neither markedly aggressive nor markedly withdrawn. It was found that the parents of the aggressive boys encouraged their children to be aggressive. The parents not only believed that boys should know how to fight and stand up for their rights but the fathers in the aggressive group tended to use physical punishment and deprivation of privileges as disciplinary techniques, whereas fathers in the control group tended to use reasoning more. Additionally, fathers in the aggressive group were less accepting of dependency from the boys than fathers in the control group.

Bandura's research has shown that children who observe aggressive or violent behavior are more likely to behave aggressively than those who do not make such observations.[69] The adult who administers corporal

---

[67]Ibid., p. 198.

[68]Bandura, A., and Walters, R.H.: *Adolescent Aggression.* New York: Ronald, 1959.

[69]Bandura, A., Ross, D., and Ross, S.A.: Imitation of film-mediated aggressive models. *Journal of Abnormal and Social Psychology, 66:* 3–11, 1963.

punishment is modeling aggression. Symbolic modeling is also effective in promoting aggression.[70] Thus children who watch aggressive behavior in films or on television are more likely to act aggressively.

Bandura designated three types of modeling behavior: the *inhibitory-disinhibitory effect*, the *eliciting effect*, and *the modeling effect*.[71] The inhibitory-disinhibitory effect renders a response less frequent or allows it to occur by influencing the response consequences of a model. Generally one becomes inhibited by observing others who experience unpleasant consequences for engaging in behavior similar to one's own. Models have an eliciting effect by influencing a response repertoire already present in the observer. An individual may have intended to help the homeless but does not do so until observing a friend involved in such activity. Finally, one develops new responses by observing a model. Children learn new behavior by observing parents, siblings, peers, and teachers.

Bandura identified four components of observational learning: *attentional, retentional, motoric, reproduction,* and *incentive,* or *motivational processes*.[72] Observers are more likely to attend to models perceived as warm, competent, and powerful. Observers who are more dependent, have lower self concepts, and/or higher anxiety are more likely to model behavior. In addition to attending, the learner must build a representation of the observed behavior that can be remembered. Retentional processes include the use of rehearsal, imagery, and elaboration. The third component, motoric reproduction, refers to the actual performance of the observed behavior. The individual must select and organize response elements and then refine the response on the basis of information feedback. The learner's self-efficacy—the belief that one can successfully execute the required behavior—influences success, as learners who lack conviction they can master a task will discontinue working on it. The fourth component, motivational processes, indicates that vicarious reinforcement and punishment provide incentives to perform behaviors that one has seen rewarded and avoid those seen punished. Reinforcement operates in observational learning largely as an antecedent rather than a consequent influence. In other words, it is important as a source of information and an incentive rather than a strengthener of behavior.

---

[70]Bandura, A., Ross, D., and Ross, S.A.: Vicarious reinforcement and imitative learning. *Journal of Abnormal and Social Psychology, 67:* 601–607, 1963.

[71]Bandura, A.: *Principles of Behavior Modification.* New York: Holt, Rinehart and Winston, 1969.

[72]Bandura, *Social Learning Theory.*

Direct reinforcement is not a necessary component of observational learning; vicarious reinforcement and self-reinforcement are identified as components. In vicarious reinforcement the model is reinforced for appropriate behavior and the observer's performance of the same behavior increases even though the observer was not directly reinforced. For example, a student who helps the teacher clean the chalkboard is directly reinforced; consequently, other students begin helping the teacher with the task. In contrast, self-reinforcement is consciously created by the individuals who develop performance standards for themselves and reward or criticize their own performances.

Bandura refers to his position in his later research as "social cognitive theory."[73] In terms of the socialization of moral judgment, parents must rely on physical guidance when the child does not understand speech; whereas social sanctions replace physical ones as children mature. Children then begin to regulate their actions on the basis of anticipated approved and disapproved conduct. Successful socialization requires the gradual substitution of internal and symbolic controls for external demands and sanctions. Parents promote discernment of moral rules not only by modeling moral judgments but by explaining the factors on which they base judgments. Standards acquired by modeling are affected by variations in the model's judgments over time and whether models practice what they profess. Models who are consistent in judging moral predicaments usually exert greater influence on children's moral reasoning than models who disagree with each other. In social cognitive theory, the effect of moral thought on conduct involves a reciprocity of influence between thought, conduct, and social factors.[74] The self-regulatory mechanism has three major subfunctions: self-monitoring of conduct; judgment of conduct in terms of personal standards and environmental circumstances; and affective self-reaction. Self-monitoring is the first step, but this must give way to a judgmental function in which the individual must integrate the morally relevant information and ascertain the weight to be given in light of multidimensional rules for judging conduct. Affective self-reactions enable standards to regulate conduct by anticipatory self-respect and self-censure for actions that violate personal standards. But there may be a discrepancy between possessing self-regulatory capabilities and the ability to apply them effectively, as

---

[73]Bandura, Albert: *Social Foundations of Thought and Action.* Englewood Cliffs, NJ: Prentice-Hall, 1986.

[74]Ibid., pp. 488–498.

self-efficacy comes into play. Self-efficacy judgments affect task selection, the level of effort and persistence, and the level of performance. The stronger the self-efficacy, the more perseverance and the greater resistance to pressures to violate moral standards.[75]

Yet people can engage or disengage their morality from humane conduct. Self-sanctions can be disengaged by reconstructing conduct, employing euphemistic language, misrepresenting or disregarding injurious consequences, and blaming and devaluating victims. Destructive behavior may be redefined as serving moral purposes. This can be observed in military conduct where people who deplore killing can be transformed into skilled combatants by redefining the morality of killing. Cognitive restructuring, however, can also be used to change inhumane conditions, as when social reformers appeal to morality to bring about social change.

Another mechanism is euphemistic language in which language is used to mask the reprehensible acts or even confer a respectable status to them. Terrorists label themselves as "freedom fighters" and bombing attacks become "clean, surgical strikes." Euphemisms are used when seeking personal benefits that harm others.

A third form of moral disengagement disregards injurious consequences by distorting or obscuring relations between actions and the harm caused. This results when personal agency is obscured and therefore responsibility is displaced. Displacement of responsibility not only weakens restraints over one's own actions but diminishes social concern over those mistreated.

Finally, by divesting victims of human qualities, self-sanctions against cruelty are blunted or nullified. This can be seen in Nazi death camps. Many aspects of contemporary life lead to depersonalization: urbanization, automation, bureaucratization, and mobility. These conditions promote anonymous and impersonal ways of relating to one another. Social practices based on ingroup and outgroup relationships also lead to estrangement.[76] In conclusion, Bandura has demonstrated the power of observational learning in complex social behavior and has made significant contributions to prosocial and deviant behavior. His theory rests on

---

[75]Bandura, Albert: Social cognitive theory of moral thought and action. In Kurtines, William M. and Gewirtz, Jacob L. (Eds.): *Handbook of Moral Behavior and Development.* Hillsdale, N.J.: Lawrence Erlbaum Associates, 1991, Vol. I, pp. 45–103.

[76]Ibid., pp. 71–103; Evans, Richard E.: *Albert Bandura: The Man and His Ideas A Dialogue.* New York: Praeger, 1989, ch. 3.

"triadic reciprocity" in which the environment, the person, and behavior are considered components of a system. Environmental influences do not strictly determine behavior but affect it through intermediary cognitive processes. Both thought and action produce self-evaluative reactions that perform a self-regulatory function. Moreover, self-efficacy is one of the most important determinants of behavior. Many of his ideas are supported by rigorous and often imaginative studies.

Bandura, however, has not developed the implications of the social dimensions with the same rigor as the learning dimensions. In formulating his model of triadic reciprocity, he neglects the work of symbolic interactionists and ethnonomethodologists. Though he does treat social diffusion, the social interaction process through which diffusion and innovation occur are not mentioned. Bandura's discussion of freedom is limited and difficult to defend when simply conceptualized as the number of behavioral options (apart from their content or consequences).

The problem that philosophers refer to as "weakness of will" is illuminated by forms of disengagement from morality and his analysis of how moral judgment is socialized. But the cognitive grounds for judging what one will do in moral dilemma situations are not well developed. Nor is it explained how moral judgment grows more sophisticated and changes over time. Nevertheless, our understanding of moral development is considerably enhanced by studies of modeling and self-efficacy.

PIAGET: COGNITIVE MORAL JUDGMENT

Possibly excepting B.F. Skinner, no psychologist has drawn as much attention during the last fifty years as Jean Piaget. The Swiss theorist's voluminous studies in genetic epistemology have made acute observations on almost every aspect of the child's development. (As will be shown, some critics are more impressed by Piaget's observational skills than they seem to be with his explanations for some peculiarly difficult concepts.)

This section treats Piaget's explicit formulation of how the child develops moral judgment. Much of Piaget's discussion on this topic is contained in his *The Moral Judgment of the Child* (1932). Later works by Piaget illustrate that his classic 1932 statement forms a consistent pattern, minor exceptions notwithstanding, with his larger theory of cognition. Given Piaget's standing in the psychological community and the fact that Kohlberg directly builds upon Piaget's theory of cognitive moral judgment, it is no accident that research on Piaget's model has been abundant. Piaget's own work and subsequent studies on his research will be considered in this section.

Piaget's stage theory assumes that cognitive and moral development proceeds hand-in-hand. He further claims that the cognitive schema and structures he describes are (a) innate; (b) invariant; (c) hierarchical; and (d) culturally universal. All these postulates are carried over into Kohlberg's research. At the same time, it is important to recognize that "children's moral judgments do not exist in a social or cultural vacuum; however spontaneous they may be in their origins, they are very much subject to direct and indirect social influences both in their rate of development and . . . in the shape they take in adulthood."[77]

Piaget's research methodology makes use of the "clinical interview" technique whereby the interviewer presents problems to the child, sees how he responds, and probes the limits of his knowledge. This method seeks to tap the child's *underlying cognitive-structural capacities,* rather than merely measure, in behavioral terms, observable surface performance. Thus there is a built-in component of speculation in Piaget's observational techniques. The clinical interview has also been called a fairly "conservative" diagnostic procedure in that the interviewer waits for the child to answer and explain *all* his responses before proceeding to more difficult operations and processes in the interview.

Not so parenthetically, the pronoun "he" is used throughout this treatment of Piaget because his study of morality included only a small sample of *male* youth, mainly from middleclass backgrounds. These children ranged in age from 5 to 13. In terms of testing moral judgment capacities, Piaget focuses on (1) how children play the game of marbles; and (2) how they respond and react to stories of moral events posed by the interviewer.

Given this research design, some critics have questioned whether Piaget is really assessing issues in moral development.[78] That is to say, Piaget seems unable to disengage implicit questions of cognitive process, particularly memory, from explicit issues in morality. Research shows that young children typically encounter difficulty in making inferences;

[77]Lickona, Thomas: Research on Piaget's theory of moral development. In Lickona (Ed.): *Moral Development and Behavior: Theory, Research, and Social Issues.* New York, Holt, Rinehart and Winston, 1976, pp. 239–240.

[78]DeVitis, Joseph L.: Cooperation and social equality in childhood: Adlerian and Piagetian lessons. *Journal of Research and Development in Education,* 17:23, 1984.

yet Piaget's experiments require them to make inferential reference. Psychoanalytic as well as social learning theory has long recognized the problem the child faces in absorbing the relational complexities in stories. Still adults seldom consider the extreme effort at focal attention by which the child may only very gradually come to assimilate and understand such complexities.[79]

In *The Moral Judgment of the Child,* Piaget details how he asks children to discriminate the "rules of the game." For example: Where do rules originate? Can they be modified? If so, when and how? How do we define lying, cheating, and "fair" punishment for transgressions? How should we distribute rewards? Should children ever contradict the authority of adults?

The latter question raises the larger philosophic discussion in Piaget's account; for a substantial portion of *Moral Judgment* is spent in a revisionist critique of Durkheim. By definition, Durkheim views education and development as the proper exercise of adult influence on "those that are not yet ready for social life."[80] Piaget intends to give greater play to the child's *own* transformations of inner perception and external reality. He implies that Durkheim has carried the traditional adult-role model of moral development to such an extent that he has been blinded to youth's potentialities:

> Durkheim thinks of children as knowing no other society than adult society or the societies created by adults (schools), so that he entirely ignores the existence of spontaneously formed children's societies, and of the facts relating to mutual respect.[81]

(Piaget's optimistic scenario of youth's spontaneity and mutual peer respect will be scrutinized later in the section.)

By contrast, Piaget's cognitive-structural approach attempts to show how sociomoral knowledge develops out of a background of authority and constraint (Durkheim) and then moves in a direction of autonomy, cooperation, and equality. In this process, Piaget posits two major stages of development:

(1)   *heteronomous morality* (or *moral realism*), in which the very young child bases his moral judgment on unilateral respect for authority figures, i.e.,

---

[79]Schachtel, Ernest: Focal attention. In Coser, Rose (Ed.): *The Family: Its Structure and Functions.* New York, St. Martin's, 1969, p. 389.

[80]Durkheim, Emile: *Education and Sociology* (1922), S.D. Fox (Tr.). Glencoe, Free Press, 1956, p. 71.

[81]Piaget, Jean: *The Moral Judgment of the Child* (1932), Marjorie Gabain (Tr.). New York, Collier, 1962, pp. 343, 356.

bases his moral judgment on unilateral respect for authority figures, i.e., "objective" rules of parents and other adults. This stage primarily reflects a *morality of constraint, absolutistic* thought patterns, and only "immanent" concepts of "fairness" and "justice."

(2)   *autonomous morality* (or a *morality of equity and cooperation*), in which the young person, by middle childhood to early adolescence, begins to develop a more "subjective" sense of autonomy and reciprocity. In this stage, social experience, principally peer interaction, becomes the main vehicle for increasingly cooperative, egalitarian growth.

Piaget claims that the young child's immature cognitive processes are severely inhibited by a lengthy period of *egocentrism*. He uses this term descriptively, not pejoratively, to characterize the relative inability to separate components of internal and external reality. In practical terms, egocentrism prevents the child from *decentering,* or placing himself in the viewpoint of another person. Thus Piaget postulates that maturation beyond egocentrism marks the beginning of all morality. It should also be noted that some recent studies on children's communication skills indicate that the child may not be so typically "egocentric" as Piaget would lead us to believe.[82]

Once the child resolves some of the difficulties inherent in distinguishing his own "reality" from the givens in external reality, Piaget foresees a more or less natural process of gradually unfolding moral development (much in the manner of Rousseau's "ripe tomato" analogy). Unless one is somehow deprived of social experiences, particularly with peers, Piaget assumes that such growth will occur. To a significant extent (perhaps more than any other theorist), Piaget argues that *peer interaction* is vital because it is the only legitimately *equal* form of moral participation. As such, he implies, on a broader level, that equality may likewise be the most legitimate testing ground for morality in general. Like Adler, Piaget also characterizes cooperations as the defining standard for both a "mature" culture and personality:

> One may conceive of cooperation as constituting the ideal form of equilibrium towards which society tends when compulsory conformity comes to break down. . . . Cooperation . . . seems to be essentially the social relation which tends to eliminate infantile phenomena. . . . [It] is the limit and norm of every human group that has ever come into being.[83]

---

[82]Donaldson, Margaret: *Children's Minds.* New York, Norton, 1978, pp. 11–25. Also: see Maratsos, Michael: Non-egocentric communication abilities in preschool children. *Child Development,* 44:697–700, 1973; and Lloyd, Peter: Communication in preschool children. Unpublished doctoral dissertation, Edinburgh University, 1975.

[83]Piaget, Jean: *The Moral Judgment of the Child,* pp. 346, 348, 371.

Nevertheless, the interactional "give-and-take" which Piaget extolls as the *sine qua non* of an "autonomous" and democratically-based morality has not been conclusively substantiated in the research literature. Bronfenbrenner observes that peer interaction in American youth leads to excessive dependence on peer approval.[84] Thus the maturing child may simply be relinquishing one form of authority for another, i.e., adult authority gives way to peer authority. Lickona has evaluated the effect of both peer interaction and the absence of adult constraint and finds mixed results:

> The evidence is strongest for the role of cognitive development, mixed but generally supportive regarding the contribution of peer experience, and weakest with respect to the role of freedom from the constraining influence of adult authority.[85]

More generally, Rosen cautions against extrapolation from Piaget's experiments since they revolve solely around the boundaries and limitations of "stories" and the "game of marbles" paradigm.[86] Though the child may appear to be gaining autonomy in certain areas of rule experience, he may well remain heteronomous in rule applications in other areas of life.

Meanwhile, Epstein has challenged Piaget's position on the ground that young children may not adequately understand the difference between "breaking" and "changing" a rule.[87] Epstein's experiments indicate that once a child is aware of the distinction, s/he is more likely to permit modifications in the rules of the game.

In its story-telling technique, Piaget's experiments often pair stories: one story tests whether the child recognizes moral *intentions* in the story characters, and the other story attempts to show whether the child can foresee *consequences* in the story development. Once again, Piaget seems to have "built in" a contaminating element in his own experimentation. In effect, he imposes "either/or" choices on the child (one for "intentions," the other for "consequences"), thus appearing to steer him in certain directions. There is also a larger question as to whether the concepts

---

[84]Bronfenbrenner, Urie: *Two Worlds of Childhood: U.S. and U.S.S.R.* New York, Sage Foundation, 1970. Also: see Hogan, Robert: Moral conduct and moral character: a psychological perspective. *Psychological Bulletin*, 79:227, 1973.

[85]Lickona, Thomas. Research on Piaget's theory of moral development, p. 240.

[86]Rosen, Hugh: *The Development of Sociomoral Knowledge: A Cognitive-Structural Approach.* New York, Columbia U.P., 1980, p. 35.

[87]Epstein, R.: The development of children's conceptions of rules in the years four to eight. Unpublished senior paper, University of Chicago, 1965.

"intention" and "consequences" can be so neatly distinguished. Finally, in cognitive developmental terms, it may be that assimilation of intention and consequences proceeds at differing rates for the very same child under experimentation. In other words, the cognitive acquisition of each process may not follow in precise or proximate tandem.

Other issues also leave the curious student of moral development with some open-ended questions about possible *alternative explanations* for Piaget's findings. May growth in morality have more to do with *experimental* influences than with logical or intellectual abilities *per se?* Might children fare better in experimentation on morality if they were more *familiar* with the *tasks* involved in such evaluation? In a related sense, do *perceptual* factors and *attentional* problems inherent in the arrangement of these tasks confuse the child and therefore yield a distorted picture of his actual capabilities? Are Piaget's explanations adequate proof for the existence of inborn cognitive schemas and structures which supposedly form the basis for evolving moral development? And does such development necessarily imply simultaneous growth in moral and cognitive judgment and action?

More positively, Piaget has at least grounded his theory of morality in *semi-observational* techniques, however limited his focus on stories and the game of marbles leaves his investigation. This is in stark contrast to Freud, Adler, and Jung, who tend to spawn their notions in airier forms of speculation. Moreover, Piaget has afforded penetrating vision for disparate schools of psychology from psychoanalytic theory, through social learning theory, to current models of cognitive structuralism. As an example, the "game of marbles" analogue generates a host of questions and issues for rule theory.[88] Piaget's descriptions and conceptualizations also help explain the construction of civilization and its attendant norms, roles, and exceptions.[89] It goes without saying that social learning theory has long been interested in rule application and modeling behavior. Cognitive-structural research in moral development might well provide richer perspectives for distinguishing how rules emerge and what constitutes appropriate modeling behavior. And, in the end, Piaget conjures up perhaps the most intriguing question of all:

---

[88]Szasz, Thomas: *The Myth of Mental Illness.* New York, Hoeber-Harper, 1961.

[89]Bettelheim, Bruno: Education and the reality principle. In Bettelheim: *Surviving and Other Essays.* New York, Vintage, 1980, p. 138.

Might a plane of *equality* be the most compelling crucible by which to assess moral judgment in its purest form?

Gruber and Vonèche conclude their analysis of Piaget's theory of moral development on an equally sobering note:

> Piaget is aware of a deep social question raised by his work. Although moral judgment develops in certain regular ways, it is by no means obvious that adult behavior lives up to the idealized norms of which children are capable. There are various plausible ways of understanding this disparity. For example, it may be that all mature adults are capable of high levels of moral judgment, but not necessarily of moral behavior, given the pressures of an often irrational and corrosive society. Or, it may be that living in such a world eventually erodes the capacity for moral judgment and even for rational thought.[90]

---

[90]Gruber, Howard E. and Vonèche, J. Jacques (Ed.): *The Essential Piaget.* New York, Basic, 1977, p. 155. For another extensive, clear account of Piaget's theory, see: Kay, William: *Moral Development: A Psychological Study of Moral Growth from Childhood to Adolescence.* London: Allen and Unwin, 1970.

Chapter 3

MORAL DEVELOPMENT IN ADOLESCENCE

HAVIGHURST: DEVELOPMENTAL TASKS

D EVELOPMENTAL tasks is a concept that was first discussed as early as 1935, was used by Erik Erikson, and culminated in a major study by Robert J. Havighurst.[1] Here Havighurst's approach to the concept will be presented.

A developmental task emerges at a certain period in an individual's life, "successful achievement of which leads to happiness and to success with later tasks, while failure leads to unhappiness in the individual, disapproval by the society, and difficulty with later tasks."[2] Developmental tasks have been formulated for infancy and early childhood, middle childhood, adolescence, early adulthood, middle age, and later maturity. Our focus will be on the adolescent period and, specifically, moral development. Though the developmental tasks differ, once understood how they function in adolescence their functions in other stages are analogous. Listed below are developmental tasks for adolescence.

1. Achieving new and more mature relations with age-mates of both sexes
2. Achieving a masculine or feminine social role
3. Accepting one's physique and using the body effectively
4. Achieving emotional independence of parents and other adults
5. Achieving assurance of economic independence
6. Selecting and preparing for an occupation
7. Preparing for marriage and family life
8. Developing intellectual skills and concepts necessary for civic competence
9. Desiring and achieving socially responsible behavior
10. Acquiring a set of values and an ethical system as a guide to behavior

---

[1]Havighurst, Robert J.: *Human Development and Education.* New York, McKay, 1953.

[2]*Ibid.,* p. 2.

50

Of the above tasks, the last two relate directly to moral development in adolescence. The notion behind this and other tasks is that they need to be achieved at the proper time to be achieved well, and the failure in one task can cause partial or complete failure in subsequent tasks. Consequently, it is important for adults to provide the conditions to facilitate appropriate task achievement.

A critical task of adolescence is to develop a mature set of values and desirable traits that would characterize the good person and the good citizen. This is a lengthy process that begins in early childhood with the emergence of conscience.

In order to fulfill the task of desiring and achieving socially responsible behavior, it is necessary to take account of society's values so that one can participate as an effective citizen in the community. To achieve this task, there are psychological and cultural bases for doing so but no biological ones. In other words, this is learned, rather than inherited, behavior that stems from society's influence upon the individual.

In terms of the psychological basis, the adolescent learns to make sacrifices for a greater good of the group, family, or community and, in turn, may be rewarded for manifesting the desired behavior. Various ceremonies, national holidays, and rituals, whether patriotic or religious, ranging from Independence Day to religious communion, help cement social bonds. Youths during late adolescence become strongly altruistic and are willing to consider the larger social good.

The cultural basis of this task can be viewed in relation to different social classes. Among the middle class, many youths may leave their local community to attend college or in search of employment and do not develop strong ties with their community. In contrast, the upper class teach their offspring the responsibility of social service, even though these teachings fail conspicuously to be absorbed by some. The lower class youth feels less responsibility to the community and relates more closely to neighbors or to an extended family structure.

To better promote this developmental task, secondary schools can teach about the life of the local community through studies of its various social, economic, and cultural features. Some appreciation for one's region and nation can be gained by reading history and biography. Ceremonies can also be used to inculcate greater loyalty to the community and nation. Additionally, youth could be encouraged to devote two or three hours daily to community work.

The other adolescent task in moral development is to acquire a set of values and an ethical system as a guide to behavior. Thus the task involves formulating a set of values capable of being realized and consciously to strive to achieve these values. This also involves keeping one's values in harmony with one's view of the world.

Havighurst holds that values form a hierarchy, and that the primary sources of all values are physiological drive. These drives—for food, warmth, physical activity, bodily stimulation—are patterned values for the infant from which other values are derived. These derived values reside in the infant's striving to gain the mother's approval and alter other adults: hence, the child learns to defer, when necessary, satisfaction of the patterned values in order to gain the deferred values. The adolescent learns desired values, according to this approach, in six ways: satisfaction of physiological drives, fulfillment of emotional experiences, consistent rewards and punishments, association of the desired value with love or approval, inculcation by an authority figure, reasoning and reflective thinking.

To help the adolescent acquire values one should recognize the role of identification and imitation and, consequently, the use of biography can be an influential source of value formation. Since youth learn desirable and undesirable values from peers, some adult supervision of these activities is needed. The study of values can be pursued through philosophy, literature, history, and art; secondary students also need to examine the scientific world view in relation to values. Not to be overlooked are ceremonies that bring youth together for an experience that offers emotional satisfaction.

Assessment of Developmental Tasks

Several hypotheses were tested, rating scales devised, and the reliability of ratings assessed.[3] It was hypothesized that good achievement on a developmental task at one age would be followed by good achievement on similar tasks at a later age; that good achievement on a developmental task is associated with good achievement on tasks at the same age; and that in a minority of cases good achievement on one task may be used to compensate for inadequate achievement on other tasks; and that there are certain personality characteristics significantly related to achieving these tasks.

---

[3]*Ibid.,* ch. 19.

The procedures used were to select five developmental tasks for study (one task was the development of conscience, morality, and a set of values); then definitions were developed of success and failure in achieving these tasks, and rating scales were devised. Reliability of ratings among the eight judges was determined by computing product-moment correlation coefficients (a basic formula for calculating the coefficient of correlation between two variables), and it was found that the average ratings of any one set of four judges had nearly the same reliability as the average of the other set of judges.

The development of conscience, morality, and a set of values was found to be rather highly related to other tasks.[4] The lowest relationship was found between emotional independence and other tasks. Another hypothesis confirmed that good performance on a task at one age is followed by good performance on this and similar tasks at a later age. The one exception is the task of learning appropriate sex roles. Considerable fluctuation in task performance occurs between the ages of 10 and 13; consequently, relationships are closer on task performance between ages 13 and 16 than ages 10 and 13. The hypothesis that some persons use good achievement in one task to compensate for inadequate achievement in another was not confirmed. As for personality traits, some were consistently related to task achievement. Those traits significantly related to the development of conscience, morality, and values for both males and females are realistic assignment of responsibility or behavior of self and others, realistic balance self-perception, and outer emotional stability.

What are the advantages and shortcomings of developmental tasks? This approach may be of help to teachers in planning objectives and a guide for parents as to what can be expected from their offspring at different developmental stages. It shows that even while human development is an individual matter, certain tasks are common to all. And it is an effective way of organizing fragmented knowledge—physical maturation, drives, motivation, emotion, and socialization. It also emphasizes the importance of timing and pacing of effort to relate activities and resources meaningfully to the appropriate developmental tasks.

One conceptual problem is that developmental tasks are said to lead to happiness when achieved and to unhappiness when failure occurs. "Happiness," however, is a weasel word that not only varies in meaning

---

[4]*Ibid.,* ch. 20. Also see: Peck, Robert F., et al.: *The Psychology of Character Development.* New York, Wiley, 1960, ch. 7.

from one culture to another but within a culture according to social class, ethnicity, religiosity, and one's philosophy of life. It may be easier to talk about unhappiness than happiness, as certain noxious conditions—unrelieved pain, a terminal illness, death of loved ones, abject poverty—are likely to cause most anyone unhappiness. Yet, even here, one can choose one's attitude toward personal misfortune, as Viktor Frankl did while incarcerated in a Nazi concentration camp.[5] Thus if developmental tasks as a concept is to be more scientifically testable, terms such as "happiness" and "unhappiness" need to be deleted and unequivocal, operational terms substituted.

While the concept of developmental tasks moves away from an individualistic needs approach and gains balance by relating the growing individual to social expectations, the task of "desiring and achieving socially responsible behavior" seems to make the group or the community the standard of behavior. This is true of some other tasks as well (e.g., the task of developing civic competence). Havighurst, especially in his examples, seems to assume that the task is what the law requires or what the community accepts. But this raises problems for youth who are reared in bigoted communities where discrimination and injustice are widespread. Thus implicit in the tasks is compliance with authority, not one of the highest moral levels (as we shall see in Chapter 5 when Kohlberg's developmental stages are presented).

The stages may also illustrate certain cultural or social class biases. One adolescent task is to prepare for marriage and family life. Yet increasingly many adolescents and young adults are choosing to remain single. Another task is that of selecting and preparing for an occupation. This task, however, is not one that upper class youths must fulfill either because of economic necessity or upper class expectations; in other words, they usually have a choice whether to prepare for a career.

The developmental tasks are not merely descriptive but are normative as well: they prescribe what the individual ought to do at each stage in order to become happy and successful. But some nations and cultures will define the tasks differently. Nazi Germany and Stalinist Russia define the task of "desiring and achieving socially responsible behavior" strikingly different than Western democracies. But adolescents growing up in those two nations, once they conform to Nazism or Stalinism, have fulfilled the developmental task as well as youth who learn the ways of

---

[5]Frankl, Viktor: *Man's Search for Meaning.* New York, Washington Square Press, 1963.

Western democracies. Thus, in this respect, the developmental tasks are an inadequate moral guide.

Havighurst's approach to the developmental tasks is to prescribe that schools should take considerable responsibility in helping the young to attain them. But what he has done is to assume a progressive stance so that those who hold different educational philosophies or theories (e.g., essentialism, perennialism, etc.) would refuse to countenance these tasks. In other words, those who believe that schools should aim only to develop cognitive abilities and not the whole person could not accept developmental tasks as formulated by Havighurst, who spends much time outlining the school's role in promoting these tasks.[6] Of course if all but the cognitive tasks are turned over to the home and other institutions and agencies, then those of other philosophical persuasions may possibly take more interest in this developmental theory.

ERIKSON: IDENTITY CRISIS AND IDEOLOGY

Erik H. Erikson is widely known for a variety of notable intellectual achievements. His psychosocial theory of development most distinctively places ego psychology in the context of socio-cultural perspectives. And his uniquely sensitive and penetrating psychohistorical analyses of such legendary figures as Gandhi and Luther have been singularly applauded. However, this section of the text will deal more directly with Erikson's theoretical contributions to the generation of ethics and morality in adolescence. Accordingly, we will focus on certain key aspects of Erikson's "Eight Stages of Man," or "life cycle," primarily Stage Five which refers to the endemic polarization involved in solving the tortuous problems of "identity" and "identity confusion." These appear to be peculiarly crucial tasks of adolescent moral development.

In his modification of Freud's theory of psychosexual development, Erikson attempts to utilize the broad resources of religion, anthropology, and other cross-cultural interdisciplinary studies. In a very real sense, he seeks to view the subjectivity of the individual with respect to larger social milieu, both cultural and transgenerational. Erikson's deeply moving, almost poetic, exposition takes on the substance of a hopeful utopian voyage in an age strewn with strife and seemingly dangerously unhinged from reliable direction.

---

[6]Havighurst: *Human Development and Education,* chs. 6, 8, 12–15.

Once again, we appear to be confronting those same dilemmas posed in Durkheim's original paradigm. It is Erikson's personal as well as scholarly mission to provide a more inclusive, universal ethical vision as opposed to the largely relativistic stance adopted by Durkheim.

According to Erikson, each individual is faced with, and must reconcile, certain recurrent fundamental problems, or conflicts, at each stage of life. These conflicts and their respective focal stages are not to be viewed as tightly compartmentalized passages in Erikson's typological scheme, i.e., there may well be overlapping in the chronology and duration of the stages. However, unless problems in each successive stage are solved, the individual may well be riddled by prior unresolved conflict throughout life. The following synopsis outlines Erikson's eight stages and the presenting problem polarities at each stage (for the sake of comparison, Freud's psychosexual stages are listed in parentheses):

1. Trust vs. mistrust (oral)
2. Autonomy vs. shame and doubt (anal)
3. Initiatie vs. guilt (genital)
4. Industry vs. inferiority (latency)
5. Identity vs. role diffusion (adolescence)
6. Intimacy vs. isolation (young adulthood)
7. Generativity vs. stagnation (middle adulthood)
8. Ego integrity vs. despair (late adulthood)

For Erikson, the adolescent's particular battle over identity and role diffusion is perhaps the most perplexing crisis in one's life (or at least it appears that way for struggling youth who have lived through that typically tumultuous period). Moreover, in our contemporary culture, Erikson insists that this struggle is even more pronounced and vexing: "The patient of today suffers most under the problem of what he should believe in and who he should—or, indeed, might—be or become; while the patient of early psychoanalysis suffered most under inhibitions which prevented him from being what and who he thought he knew he was."[7]

In adolescence, the maturing individual is confronted with the following confusing, conflictual identity polarizations which Erikson maintains must be balanced if s/he is to sustain epigenetic growth:

(a) Time perspective vs. time diffusion
(b) Self-certainty vs. identity consciousness

---

[7]Erikson, Erik H.: *Childhood and Society,* 2nd ed. New York, Norton, 1963, p. 279.

(c) Role experimentation vs. negative identity
(d) Anticipation of achievement vs. work paralysis
(e) Sexual identity vs. bisexual diffusion
(f) Leadership polarization vs. authority diffusion
(g) Ideological polarization vs. diffusion of ideals[8]

Once one considers the myriad changes facing the adolescent at this stage of development, the reasons for the inevitability of "identity crisis" and role confusion become clearly evident. Physiological and libidinal changes make youth feel threatened by those same peers whom they increasingly seek out for recognition—at the very time that ego and superego processes are also becoming intensified. There is a concurrent tendency to identify with "heroic" figures, to wage war in some romantic ideological cause, to belong to a social group at all costs: "What the individual has learned to see in himself must now coincide with the expectations and recognitions which others bestow on him."[9] Nor have career choice and the mastery of intellectual and affective competencies been fully articulated or accomplished. Finally, there is a compelling need to balance the "sameness and continuities" of one's past with a less defined, more unsettling future in which one cannot be certain of one's aims or the likely routes for their achievement.

To quote one of Erikson's aphorisms about the perils of the adolescent's plight: "I ain't what I ought to be, I ain't what I'm going to be, but I ain't what I was."[10] Thus the underlying goal of adolescence is to harmonize one's past and future through a fuller integration of ego identity.

Yet these efforts do not always meet with instantaneous harmony or successful adaptation. Sometimes youth, as in the case of the Beatniks of the 1950s or the Hippies of the 1960s, opt to rebel against past identities, seeing themselves as outside the restrictive codes of conduct promulgated by adult authorities. Such youth may embody what Erikson terms *negative identity,* i.e., "a desperate attempt at regaining some mastery in a situation in which available positive identity elements cancel each

---

[8]Erikson, Erik H.: Identity and the life cycle: Selected papers. In *Psychological Issues* (Monogr.). New York, International Universities, 1959, p. I:1.

[9]Erikson, Erik H.: *Insight and Responsibility: Lectures on the Ethical Implications of Psychoanalytic Insight.* New York, Norton, 1964, p. 90.

[10]Erikson, Erik H.: In M.J.E. Senn (Ed.): *Symposium on the Healthy Personality.* New York, Macy Foundation, 1950, p. 139.

other out."[11] However, any attempt to establish identity, even "negative" identity, is better than having no identity at all. In this regard, for example, Erikson speaks in sympathetic tones of Black Muslim and Black Power advocates who seek to surmount conditions of "inaudibility, invisibility, namelessness, facelessness."[12]

Some relief from the traumatic experiences of adolescence is provided by what Erikson sees as a *moratorium* period—a psychosocial, culturally accepted delay of adulthood which is somewhat analogous to Freud's concept of latency, i.e., a protective release from quickened libidinal interest. In American culture, extended forms of education, military service, and living at home with one's parents afford outlets for such a moratorium. (Of course, this moratorium may also be welcomed by the culture as a "benevolent" way to "cool off the economy," that is, keeping students out of the labor market.) In any case, this "safety valve" allows youth to step back from more active confusion, to take some perspective, and to partake of "provocative playfulness" in socially sanctioned ways.

The special fashion in which adolescents typically invest their energies is articulated in Erikson's use of the concepts *ideology* and *fidelity*. Erikson characterizes ideology as "a systematized set of ideas and ideals which unifies the striving for psychosocial identity in the coming generation, and it remains a stratum in every man's imagery, whether it remains a 'way of life' or becomes a militant 'official' ideology."[13] In this confusing attempt to establish a set of values and beliefs, Erikson insists that adolescents adopt a particular kind of moral virtue, i.e., *fidelity*, or "the ability to sustain loyalties freely pledged in spite of the inevitable contradictions of value systems."[14] Fidelity serves to "confirm" ideologies, and Erikson contends that the force of affiliation with one's peers is as important in this confirmation as any "truth" in the ideology. (Except for Piaget, no other theorist than Erikson focuses so acutely on the role of peer interaction in establishing and maintaining value systems.)

The prevalence of ideology in adolescence is a form of *ritualization*, a concept which is also vital to any understanding of Erikson's description of the evolution of morals and ethics. "Ritualization" denotes those

---

[11]Erikson, Erik H.: The problem of ego identity. *Journal of the American Psychoanalytic Association*, 4:88, 1956.

[12]Erikson, Erik H.: *Identity: Youth and Crisis.* New York, Norton, 1968, pp. 25–27.

[13]Erikson, Erik H.: Psychosocial identity. In *International Encyclopedia of the Social Sciences*, vol. VII. New York, Macmillan, 1968, p. 63.

[14]Erikson, Erik H.: *Insight and Responsibility*, p. 125.

ceremonial habits of everyday behavior which allow humans to lead balanced, adaptive lives while being affirmed by their fellows. In adolescence the ritualization of ideology customarily becomes transformed into a *totalism,* a zealous devotion to "black-and-white" standards of right and wrong in the name of some fanatical ideal. Of course, Erikson postulates that this circumstance is a fairly natural event which tends to balance out during the course of one's life cycle.

At this point it seems appropriate to show how Erikson distinguishes "morals" from "ethics." The former term is more akin to "infantile morality" or "adolescent ideology;" whereas the latter term is synonymous with a "letting go" of puerile values which harbor any semblance of righteousness, prejudice, or similar kinds of moralism.[15] For Erikson, a more "mature" and "universal" form of ethics disavows moralistic fanaticism of any sort because, in his words, "you can always be sure that the loudest moralists have made deals with their own consciences."[16] In essence, Erikson divides the task of ethical development into three distinct realms: (1) *moral learning* in childhood; (2) *ideological experimentation* in adolescence; and (3) *ethical consolidation* in adulthood.[17]

Erikson also provides an impressionistic thumbnail sketch of various sub-species of morality: (a) a *premoral* position is equated with a denial of any need for morality; (b) an *amoral* position "flaunts accepted norms"; (c) an *antimoral* position "militantly negates all authority"; and (d) an *anti-authoritarian,* yet moralistic, position "condemns the adult world with righteous fervor."[18] Needless to say, Erikson is searching for a more all-encompassing, universalistic morality than any of those listed above.

Erikson's most mature delineation of the ethical realm is couched in "a universal sense of values assented to."[19] His analysis tends to base itself in the bedrock values common to all the great major religions of the world. In particular, it is largely quilted from the Judeo-Christian faith in the Golden Rule: "love thy neighbor as thyself." Erikson reformulates this rule in accordance with his notion of *mutuality,* in which devotion to

[15]Erikson, Erik H.: *Identity: Youth and Crisis,* pp. 119–120; 259–260.

[16]Erikson, Erik H.: *Life History and the Historical Moment.* New York, Norton, 1975, p. 22. See also Erikson, Erik H.: *Dimensions of a New Identity: The 1973 Jefferson Lectures in the Humanities.* New York, Norton, 1974, pp. 108, 114–117.

[17]Erikson, Erik H.: *Life History and the Historical Moment,* p. 206.

[18]Erikson, Erik H.: Reflections on the dissent of contemporary youth. *Daedalus,* 99:165, Winter, 1970.

[19]Erikson, Erik H.: *Life History and the Historical Moment,* p. 207.

the other reconciles "the antagonisms inherent in divided function."[20] That is to say, Erikson admonishes that "what is hateful to yourself, do not to your fellow man."[21] In the final analysis, then, Erikson's ideal form of ethical action would produce "mutuality between the doer and the other."[22] Such a vision is reminiscent of the moral programs of Gandhi and Martin Luther King, Jr. Thus, for Erikson, as for Adler, personal growth and communal change are of one piece; and the crisis of identity cannot be artificially separated from historical development and commitment among generations past, present, and future.

Nevertheless, Erikson's almost messianic call for universalism has often run up against harsher barriers in actual human history. Countless social groups, classes, religions, and nations have practiced what Erikson terms a *pseudo-species mentality*. The bearers of ideological sovereignty are typically consumed with false pride and an unquenchable belief in the power and immortality of their group's ideas and ideals. From the Inquisition to Nazi Germany and Jonestown, such world views have been known to lead to destruction, bloody tragedy, and unfulfilled hopes. For example, it may be no coincidence that most wars have been fought in the name of nationalism or religious intent.

These realistic considerations tend to leave Erikson's well-intentioned effort to articulate clinical psychological observation in a sort of moralistic, exhortative vacuum of its own. Erikson would like to claim that he grounds his ethical stance not "on the moral injunction of avoiding affront to the ideal but on the ethical capacity to provide strength in the actual."[23] Yet Erikson, like Adler, is also guilty of a form of naturalistic fallacy in his own argumentation. As Paul Roazen, perhaps Erikson's most perceptive critic, puts it: "The problem is that Erikson does not seem sufficiently aware of the logical dilemma in moving from empirical statements to value judgments, in inferring an 'ought' from an 'is.' "[24]

---

[20]Erikson, Erik H.: *Identity: Youth and Crisis,* p. 219.

[21]Erikson, Erik H.: *Insight and Responsibility,* p. 243.

[22]Erikson, Erik H.: The golden rule and the cycle of life. In White, Robert (Ed.): *The Study of Lives: Essays in Honor of Henry A. Murray.* New York, Atherton, 1963, p. 423.

[23]Erikson, Erik H.: *Insight and Responsibility,* p. 177.

[24]Roazen, Paul: *Erik H. Erikson: The Power and Limits of a Vision.* New York, Free, 1976, p. 119. Roazen's analysis is especially helpful in applying social critique to Erikson's treatment of morality. For a more sympathetic view of Erikson, see Wright, J. Eugene, Jr.: *Erikson: Identity and Religion.* New York, Seabury, 1982. Recently, feminist criticism has been less sympathetic to Erikson's controversial notion of "inner space," which posits that female personality development is confined by the "groundplan" of the womb. See Okin, Susan Moller: *Women in Western Political Thought,* Princeton, Princeton U.P., 1980, pp. 238–241.

Implicit in Roazen's critique is a more grievous gap in Erikson's own utopian agenda: the serious neglect of policy recommendations to implement social and institutional change. In many ways, Erikson's soothing ego psychology amounts to an adjustment psychology which might serve to cushion men's acceptance of the status quo. In the end, using his own poetical language, Erikson's ideology may thus be seen as a credo brightly shining in the night—but one which is disabled in the deployment of powerful social and political rudders.

PACKER: HERMENEUTICS AND MORAL ACTION

Hermeneutics is a contemporary European school of thought with lengthy roots in the past. It challenges behavioral and constructivist approaches in psychology in terms of its basic theoretical assumptions and framework of inquiry. Hermeneutics has been defined in at least six different ways (in roughly chronological order) as: (1) the theory of biblical exegesis; (2) general philological methodology; (3) the science of all linguistic understanding; (4) the methodology foundation of *Geisteswissenschafen* (all disciplines focused on understanding art, actions, and writings); (5) phenomenology of existence and of existential understanding; and (6) systems of interpretation used to uncover meaning behind myths and symbols.[25]

Martin J. Packer has conducted research on the structure of moral action and conflict by using a hermeneutic approach.[26] Packer follows Heidegger's philosophical interpretation of hermeneutics as the phenomenology of existence and existential understanding.[27] Moreover, Packer considers his approach analytic hermeneutics, which is distinct from but rests on ontological hermeneutics. Analytic hermeneutics examines the way activity is organized in a particular type of local setting, whereas ontological hermeneutics seeks to uncover and articulate the basic structures of human existence.

---

[25]Palmer, Richard E.: *Hermeneutics,* Evanston, IL: Northwestern University Press, 1969, p. 33.

[26]Packer, Martin J.: *The Structure of Moral Action: A Hermeneutic Study of Moral Conflict.* Basel: Karger, 1985; Social interaction as practical activity: Implications for the study of social and moral development. In Kurtines, William M. and Gewirtz, Jacob L. (Eds.): *Moral Development through Social Interaction.* New York, Wiley, 1987, pp. 245–277; Packer and Richardson, Ellen: Analytic hermeneutics and the study of morality in action. In Kurtines, William M. and Gewirtz, Jacob L. (Eds.): *Handbook of Moral Behavior and Development.* Hillsdale, N.J.: Lawrence Erlbaum, 1991, vol. 1, pp. 335–371.

[27]Heidegger, Martin: *Being and Time.* New York: Harper & Row, 1927/1962.

Packer adopts Heidegger's distinction between three modes of engagement in human activity. The ready-to-hand mode characterizes our everyday involvement with tools, paraphernalia, and other people. This mode is structured by our concerns and moods as we act, but it is not instrumental in the sense of employing means-ends planning.

The unready-to-hand mode arises whenever some problem or breakdown occurs in our unreflective conduct. Where before the situation was not distinct, now various aspects are highlighted and instrumental strategies are initiated to alleviate the difficulty.

The present-at-hand mode is one of detached reflection and contemplation in which theorizing and philosophical discussion occur. This mode arises when we are unable to find direct solutions to a problem or a breakdown. In contrast, hermeneutic inquiry initially operates in the first two modes.

Packer believes that nonrational elements, such as emotions, should be interpreted in moral action despite the tendency in psychology for a privileged place to be reserved for logic over feeling, rationality over emotions. The empiricist approach to emotions emphasizes impulsive reaction and the rationalist approach stresses cognitive appraisal. The first approach breaks the phenomena of emotions into components and links them in a causal manner; whereas the second approach takes similar components and links them by rule-following cognition. Both theories, Packer claims, treat emotion in almost entirely an epiphenomenal role to the experiential character of an emotion. The essential problem of both theories is that it renders the experience of emotion unnecessary and therefore leaves it largely unanalyzed.

Packer holds that emotions may occur prior to rational processes of perception and evaluation. Emotion plays a structuring and organizing role by focusing our experiences in particular ways. With each emotion objects display qualities in a newly perceived manner and possibilities for action are highlighted. Strong emotions move us to certain forms of action, but emotions are experienced as having their source from within. Emotion arises when something challenges the individual by affecting the person's interests; it transforms one's relation to the world by requiring the individual to deal with changes in the world. Emotions confront us with our facticity, and moods enable us to direct our will and to think about a fact or state of affairs. Since hermeneutics seeks direct access to human phenomena, emotions and moods are of critical importance in any investigation.

Social action, he states, is organized semantically by the meanings people find in social events and action, rather than in terms of material causation or logical necessity. Human actions may be understood in a variety of ways depending upon perspective and context. We can attempt to make sense out of social exchanges, which are complex and confusing, through an inductive approach.

The analytic task of hermeneutics is to that of characterizing ready-to-hand activity and describe shifts between it and the unready-to-hand mode of engagement. The ready-to-hand activity is our primary origin of our understanding the social world.

Packer has studied exchanges between infant and adult, kindergarten children, and adolescents/young adults. The latter study involves a moral conflict among participants (modal age 19 years) engaged in a modified version of the Prisoner's Dilemma game.[28] Video recordings were made of teams in order to explore several occasions when an agreement to cooperate was made and broken by the team winning the most points.

The methodological focus was on the intimacy among participants and on the social and moral stances adopted. In playing the game, within a short time one team had more points; the losing team soon became bored and frustrated. Team members agreed then that they would play cooperatively; however, in 4 out of 10 sessions the winners broke the agreement and gained more points. The participants called the breaking of the agreement "burning." The winning team was unaware that burning would appear immoral to the losing team, as they merely took it for granted as part of the game.

Thus in the first phase the losing team expressed strong emotion (shock, surprise, confusion, moral indignation) over the burning. The winning team was identified as the transgressors. The second phase resulted in an impasse where the winning team wanted to resume the game, whereas the losing team wanted reparation for the moral wrong. Accounts of what occurred are characterized by certitude and egocenteredness. The issues are more fully addressed in the third phase but now the formulation has changed from a transgressor-transgressed relationship to a recognition of different ways of understanding events. Distance between the groups has diminished and they begin playing the

---

[28]Packer, *Structure of Moral Action.*

game again without further burning, though some residual uncertainty remains.

Packer refers to the response to the breakdown after the burning as involving practical deliberation: a way of understanding that purports to be neutral and objective but is actually organized in terms of the interests and concerns of participants. A consequence of viewing social inter-action as practical activity is to view deliberation as a social activity that begins with previous interaction and is directed toward pragmatic persuasive purposes rather than theorizing or logical argumentation (Heidegger's present-at-hand mode). Breakdown inevitably occurs in lengthy and complex social interactions and this motivates partici-pants to move from ready-to-hand mode to the unready-to-hand. These breakdowns are different than intellectual conflicts because they are embedded in practical social activity and structured by interests and concerns.

Packer's hermeneutic approach offers an alternative to dominant modes of inquiry. It recognizes the role of ongoing experience, provides a substantial place for the emotions, focuses on practical deliberation, and offers an explanation for moral conflict.

Whether Heidegger should be the principal philosophical source for such inquiry is open to question, however. Heidegger largely has aban-doned traditional logic and his writings are in constant danger of becom-ing undisciplined where passion and conviction substitute for demon-stration and obscurity is passed off as profundity. His writings are extremely obscure, not just because he deals with abstract and ultimate questions but by his highly idiosyncratic use of language in producing his own vocabulary and exploiting terminology. Habermas would likely provide a stronger foundation for a system of hermeneutics.[29] Gadamer, who was influenced by Heidegger, has developed a more comprehensive and explanatory system. Habermas, while critiquing Gadamer's approach, has sought to combine both empirical and hermeneutical forms of research.

Packer states that emotions may occur prior to rational processes of perception and evaluation. Nevertheless, he believes they play a structur-ing role by displaying qualities and highlighting possibilities for action. That emotions may arise prior to rational processes may frequently

---

[29]Gadamer, Georg: *Truth and Method.* New York: Sheed and Ward, 1975; Habermas' critique of Gadamer's view is presented in: Holub, Robert C.: *Jurgen Habermas: Critic in the Public Sphere.* New York: Routledge, 1991, ch. 3.

occur, but Packer's emphasis is largely placed on the irrationality of emotions. This does not leave much place for emotions in the service of the individual rather than merely a force that impels action.

It would be more useful for both research and therapeutic purposes to consider emotions as informing us and others of our concerns: what delights, frustrates, and distresses us in carrying out our intentions and achieving our goals. Whether a situation will evoke an emotion depends on the individual's past experience, interpretation of the situation, and how the situation may impede or facilitate the achievement of goals. The expression of emotion does not presuppose language, but knowing how to ascribe emotional behavior and discuss, analyze, and evaluate emotions presupposes a form of public discourse. And to change emotions, it is necessary to engage in thinking.

HOFFMAN: EMPATHY AND SOCIAL COGNITION

Moral development theory has generally focused on cognitive development rather than the affective domain. A notable exception, however, is the work of Martin L. Hoffman, who has conducted extensive research on empathy and its role in moral action, all of which has led to a better understanding of this relatively neglected domain.

Hoffman holds that a moral issue arises when people's goals, plans, or expectations are in conflict. Sensitivity to the rights and welfare of others, especially when they conflict with one's own interest, are central features of the moral domain. His studies involve moral conflict when either (1) one is an innocent bystander and witnesses someone in a needful state and experiences conflict between the motive to help the victim and egoistic motives not to become involved; or (2) one is not innocent but has acted or contemplates acting in a harmful way and experiences conflict between egoistic motives and feelings of obligation to help someone. Thus moral action is an attempt to achieve a balance between egoistic and moral motivation. Moral affect is the good feeling that arises from acting morally, while guilt or bad feeling is experienced from violating a moral norm.[30]

Considerable empirical evidence shows that empathic distress and guilt

---

[30]Hoffman, Martin L.: Empathy, its limitations, and its role in a comprehensive moral theory. In Kurtines, William M. and Gewirtz, Jacob L. (Eds.): *Morality, Moral Behavior, and Moral Development.* New York: Wiley, 1984, pp. 283–302.

function as moral motives in dispositions to moral action.[31] Empathy, though an affect, has a significant cognitive component, as older children and adults draw from self-knowledge and knowledge about others as to what the other is feeling. Hoffman's schema provides four developmental levels of empathy: Global empathy; "egocentric" empathy; empathy for another's feelings; and empathy for another's experiences beyond the immediate situation.

Global empathy relates to infants and their experiences of empathic distress through simple arousal modes before they acquire a sense of others as distinct from themselves. Distress cues may engender action based on what happened to others happened to themselves.

Egocentric empathy arises at about one year of age when the child's awareness of others becomes physically distinct from the self, and empathic distress can be transferred to others. The child may distinguish that someone else is in distress, but the other person's internal state may be assumed to be the same as that of the child's.

Empathy for another's feelings emerges at about two to three years of age when the child recognizes that others' feelings differ from his or her own and are based on different needs and perspectives. Children become able to empathize with a wide range of emotion as language is acquired. Children may not only empathize with a victim's distress but even someone's desire not to be helped.

Empathy for another's life condition arises in late childhood as the child recognizes the separate identities of others and becomes aware that others experience pleasure and pain not only in present situations but in larger life experiences. Thus the child can respond not only to immediate distress but the emphatic response becomes intensified upon realization that the other's distress is chronic. The child is capable of conceptualizing another's level of distress or deprivation and thereby can form social concepts about groups or classes of people, such as the poor, handicapped, disadvantaged, or homeless.[32]

As the image of the other emerges, a wish arises, though not necessarily conscious, to terminate the unpleasant affect upon oneself as well as

---

[31]Hoffman, Martin L.: Empathy: its development and prosocial implications. In Keasey, C.B. (Ed.), *Nebraska Symposium on Motivation,* Lincoln: University of Nebraska Press, 1978, vol. 25; and his Affect and moral development. In Ciccheti and Hesse, P. (Eds.), *New Directions for Child Development: Emotional Development.* San Francisco, Jossey-Bass, 1982, No. 16.

[32]Hoffman, Martin L.: Empathy, social cognition, and moral education. In Garrod, Andrew (Ed.): *Approaches to Moral Development.* New York: Teachers College Press, 1993, pp. 157–179.

the other's distress. Other causal attributions are possible. When victims are perceived as responsible for their own distress, the observer may become indifferent or derogate victims. But if the observer believes that the victim was attacked, they may sympathize with the victim or empathize as though they feel attacked themselves. When no clear cues are present of the victim's plight, the observer may blame the victim to reduce the observer's distress.

Hoffman clarifies the role of guilt in empathic distress and distinguishes it from a conditioned anxiety response to punishment and from Freudian guilt. He conceptualizes it as an interpersonal guilt that stems from an awareness of harming someone. Infants can only experience rudimentary guilt feelings, but once young children can identify others as separate agents, their empathic distress can be transformed into guilt when they perceive that they hurt someone else. And when the child recognizes that others have internal states, the empathic distress experienced when recognizing another as having painful internal states may elicit guilt feelings whenever one's actions are personally construed as responsible for those states. When other persons can be perceived as having an identity beyond the immediate situation, one's empathic response for their misfortune may be transformed into guilt by considering oneself responsible for the other's plight, or by contrasting one's relatively advantaged position in relation to another person. But even when children have acquired the developmental requisites of guilt, they may not experience it unless a parent or other adult compels them to attend to the harm done; consequently, parental discipline plays an important role in guilt feelings.[33]

Socialization contributes to empathy in a number of ways. First, socialization practices that provide an opportunity to experience many emotions would promote empathic capability because people empathize better with others' emotions when they have had the emotion themselves. Second, empathic development is fostered by attending to the internal states of others. This ability is promoted by parental discipline employing induction in which the parent draws attention to injury or pain caused another or encourages the child to imagine how the other person feels. Third, role-playing increases children's attention to others and thereby extends their empathetic capability. Fourth, children who receive consid-

---

[33]Hoffman, M.L.: Development of prosocial motivation: Empathy and guilt. In Eisenberg, N. (Ed.): *The Development of Prosocial Behavior.* New York: Academic Press, 1982, pp. 281–313.

erable attention themselves would be able to be more involved in others'
needs rather than in their own. Finally, empathic responsiverness is
fostered by models who engage in prosocial behavior and verbalize their
empathic feelings.[34]

Hoffman has also sought to determine the connection between empathy and moral principles. A commitment to a moral principle and its
impartial application should operate to reduce bias of any empathic
affect. The arousal of empathic affect may activate moral principles. In
other words, either the empathic affects may be aroused first followed by
the moral principles or they may be evoked independently. Either way, a
bond may be developed between them. Thus when the moral principle is
activated in the future, an associated empathic affect arises; therefore,
where once the moral principle was stored in memory in a "cool" didac-
tic context, it now has acquired an affectively-changed representation or
"hot" cognition. What is represented with a "hot" cognition are the
principle, empathic affect, and events from the person's life when the
principle was violated. Hot cognitions also have implications for memory because affect is a powerful retrieval cue, and if moral principles are
part of semantically organized categories of knowledge and categorical
knowledge endures in memory, hot cognitions will long be maintained
in memory.[35]

Hoffman's studies of empathy contribute vitally to a field that has
emphasized the cognitive domain more exclusively. His studies explain
the growth and development of empathy, the relation of guilt and
empathetic affect, causal attributions for empathic distress, the mechanisms to promote greater empathy, and the connection between empathy
and moral principles.

Some situations, however, involving the alleged latter connection are
problematic. For instance, in cases of youth who become involved in
delinquent gangs and manifest greater empathic distress over gang members who are apprehended for violations than over their own family
misfortunes, one might erroneously attempt to explain the behavior as
insufficient linkage between moral principles and empathetic affects.
This line of reasoning is a mistake, however, insofar as the delinquent
youths exhibit the moral principles of trust and loyalty to gang members.

---

[34]Ibid.

[35]Hoffman, Martin L.: Empathy, social cognition, and moral action. In Kurtines, William M. and
Gewirtz, Jacob L.: *Handbook of Moral Behavior and Development.* Hillsdale, NJ: Lawrence Erlbaum, 1991,
vol. 1, pp. 275–301.

Here we have a conflict, among other things, between lower and higher moral principles. Hoffman's theory, in such situations, does not indicate how empathic affects may overcome waywardness and promote desirable moral behavior.

Empathy also does not explain how children learn to achieve a proper balance between concern for others and egoistic motives. Nor does the theory relate to a morality of justice or a morality of duty. An empathic morality does not contribute to making appropriate moral judgments when behaviors are to be compared and moral claims assessed. Finally, though people can empathize at times with strangers, they are more likely to empathize with kin. A moral system, however, requires an impartial adjudication in determining moral obligations and settling moral claims.

Chapter 4

MORAL DEVELOPMENT
AND HIGHER EDUCATION

THE college years make lasting impressions upon many students—friendships formed, social life enjoyed, studies pursued, memorable professors, and growth in maturity and understanding. But what specific effect does the college experience have upon the student's values and moral development? ("College" refers throughout to the undergraduate years, whether in a college or university.) Does it merely reinforce and stabilize the values of entering freshmen, or does it bring about lasting value changes of a certain type? Does the college experience lead to growth in moral development, or is moral development similar to what early psychologists regarded about I.Q. scores—that the maximum potential is reached by age sixteen? What theories would best help to explain moral development among this age group?

Thus this chapter focuses on different theories of moral development in the college years and the body of data-based research about how higher education affects or does not affect moral development. Among those surveyed are such diverse thinkers and researchers as Philip E. Jacob, Arthur Chickering, William Perry, Douglas Heath, and Kenneth Keniston.

JACOB: VALUE CHANGE AND CURRICULUM

A pivotal point of heightened interest in the impact of college on student values occurred with the Jacob study.[1] This study's controversial findings led subsequent researchers to seek to confirm or refute them. The study was conducted to discover the effects of general education in the social sciences on the values of American college students. Jacob reviewed several hundred studies since 1920, visited 30 institutions, and gathered evaluative data on courses and curriculum at these and other institutions.

---

[1]Jacob, Philip E.: *Changing Values in College.* New York; Harper, 1957.

He found the values of the American college student "remarkably homogeneous" and the students themselves "gloriously contented," "unabashedly self-centered," and "politically irresponsible." Traditional moral values are held by most students although, as in the case of academic dishonesty, they do not always feel bound by them. Students are dutiful toward citizenship responsibilities insofar as they expect to obey laws, pay taxes, and vote, but are largely "politically illiterate." Students predict another major war within a dozen years but give little attention to international affairs. The above profile would be characteristic of 75–80 percent of American college students surveyed.

The principle effect of a college education is to bring about a general acceptance of a shared body of attitudes and standards from the college experience. More consistency in values among students can be discerned among seniors than freshmen. Thus the overall effect is to socialize the student and refine his or her values. College is a selective process to begin with, as many who have divergent attitudes do not attend and those who find the experience uncongenial drop out (up to 50 percent at the time of the study).

One of the most significant features is that student values did not substantially change as a result of the curriculum, whether enrolled in a conventional liberal arts program, an integrated general education curriculum, or a professional-vocational program. Even when the curriculum was redesigned to confront students with personal and social value issues, it rarely engendered a significant difference in beliefs, much less in their conduct.

Moreover, the quality of teaching has little effect on value outcomes in general education. The effect of the good teacher is indistinguishable from the poor one in terms of influence on values. Nor does it make much difference what teaching method is employed, though students become more involved and concerned when they are asked to confront value issues and make decisions.[2] Although students alter their opinions on many issues and become more tolerant of those with different views, college has a socializing rather than a liberalizing effect on values. "The values with which they arrive and which are integral elements of their personality, are still there when most students leave."[3]

---

[2]*Ibid.*, ch. 1.

[3]*Ibid.*, p. 53.

Jacob examined a wide range of research, but the studies' conclusions have been lumped together even though the studies use diverse methods, differently formulated problems, and were conducted by researchers of different abilities. Moreover, he gives no greater weight to important longitudinal studies than to simple comparisons between students exposed or not exposed to a human relations course. Nor does Jacob explore the number of professors who firmly believe that academic life should serve strictly intellectual purposes and who have no interest in values other than those embodied in their own discipline.

In the decade following the Jacob study (published in 1957), a voluminous literature appeared based on seeking answers to more specific and more complex questions. Researchers sought to determine the learning conditions, types of students, and the specific ways students changed. This meant looking at the college's public image, institutional size, the college environment, and other variables that interact with one another. Twelve years after the Jacob study Feldman and Newcomb concluded, after an examination of four decades of research studies, that "there are conditions under which colleges have had (and, we assume, will continue to have) impacts upon their students, and not least upon students' values. Moreover, the consequences of these impacts often persist after the college years."[4]

CHICKERING: EDUCATION AND INTEGRITY

Arthur W. Chickering has sought to synthesize research and theory in higher education in order to develop a conceptual framework faithful to the findings and relevant to a wide variety of decisions.[5] To accomplish these tasks, he has described seven vectors or major dimensions of development during the college years—competence, emotions, autonomy, identity, interpersonal relationships, purpose, and integrity. He relates these vectors to six major aspects of the college environment: objectives; institutional size; curriculum, teaching, and evaluation; residence hall arrangements; faculty and administration; friends, groups, and student culture.

Our interest lies primarily with the vector of "developing integrity"

[4]Feldman, Kenneth A. and Newcomb, Theodore M.: *The Impact of College on Students.* San Francisco, Jossey-Bass, 1969, vol. 1, p. 4.

[5]Chickering, Arthur W.: *Education and Identity.* San Francisco, Jossey-Bass, 1969.

because it pertains to values and standards; however, a brief statement about the other vectors will help clarify Chickering's framework. The vector of "developing competence" concerns intellectual, physical and manual skills, and social and interpersonal relationships. Underlying one's ability to develop competence in these areas is confidence in problem-solving and ability to achieve one's goals.

"Managing emotions," a second vector, is a task not completed by the end of secondary school, especially with problems of aggression, sexuality, and attitudes toward authority of home and community. One task is to lessen repression of the earlier years, learn to accept early feelings as legitimate emotions, gain greater self-awareness, flexible control, and freedom of expression.

"Becoming autonomous" means to become emotionally independent and instrumentally independent. The former means that one becomes free of the constant need for reassurance and approval; the latter refers to the ability to solve problems independently and remain flexible in relation to one's desires and needs.

These previous three vectors help one in the process of "establishing identity." Here the individual discovers those experiences that establish a rhythm so that self-destructive patterns are avoided; it also concerns the clarification of various aspects of ourselves—from the physical to the interpersonal. A sense of identity helps promote change in other vectors of development.

"Freeing interpersonal relationships" means to develop greater tolerance for a diversity of human behavior, increased ability to relate to others as persons rather than stereotypes. Here there is also a shift away from dependence upon close friends to interdependence.

The developmental vector of "clarifying purpose" involves seriously raising and attempting to answer such questions as "Who am I?" "What am I going to be?" "Where am I going?" One needs to deal with these questions in three areas: recreational and avocational interests, vocational plans and aspirations, and general life-style considerations. By developing purpose, the individual is able to integrate these three areas and thereby imbue one's life with greater meaning.

Returning to the vector of "developing integrity," it is related to establishing identity and clarifying purposes because one strives for an internally consistent set of beliefs and values that guide behavior. Most researchers indicate a change toward increased liberalism during the college years; the changes usually involve not so much relinquishing one value for another as that of gradually modifying the values brought to college. Thus college may more likely affect the basis for holding values, how they are held, and the role they play in one's life. Chickering insists that it is more important for values to have a larger role in the student's life than to change the content of values. The tasks are to humanize and personalize values and develop congruence among them.

Carrying out these tasks involves developing objective analyses of different conditions and learning to estimate the consequences of various alternatives. Religious values developed in the home may also come under scrutiny. By humanizing values they may become relative to differing circumstances which, in turn, may generate anxiety and a search for deeper moorings and commitment. Integrity arises when the inconsistencies between belief and deed become minimal so that once the ramifications of a situation are grasped, the response is determined. But achieving congruence is a lifelong task and the individual will need to develop new sources of strength as his support system of friends changes and new relations are formed.

Chickering explores six college environmental conditions or variables that make a difference in student development (these conditions were mentioned earlier). While all of these conditions or variables have the potential to influence student development, Chickering cites residence hall arrangements and faculty-student interaction as having an especially important impact upon values.

Friendships in residence halls are first established by propinquity and the architectural arrangement of living units. Experiences with roommates and friends help reduce ethnocentrism and promote greater acceptance of others. These changes for students are not always easy: placed in a position where one must learn to live with others and in which others could hardly be ignored, accommodation is learned, followed gradually by tolerance and acceptance of others. But as enrollment increases or institutions become more selective in admissions, opportunities for a genuine residential community may be diminished. Yet these changing conditions do not diminish the need for more lasting social relations, which are necessary to provide a sense of identity and emotional support in everyday life.

Chickering recommends that residential units become reference groups for their members whereby they convey meaningful norms and standards. This goal can best be accomplished by permitting students to live in the same unit as long as they desire; keep the size of the unit small enough so that each individual can have some impact on the whole; let students choose their own living space within the unit; and provide each residence unit operating funds for which they will be held accountable at the end of each semester.[6]

Students need both models and anti-models to develop their values. They need a distinctive college environment, professors with strong value commitments, and personal value experiences which can be integrated with their educational development. The antimodels are those whom students actively reject—the tyrant, the crowd-pleaser, haranguer, and others. The characteristics of faculty that help students to develop not only competence but purpose and values are accessibility, professors with well-integrated values, professors knowledgeable not only of their discipline but of student developmental problems, and the ability to converse with and listen effectively to students.[7]

What, then, can be said of Chickering's approach to moral development by way of summary and assessment? Chickering, by use of vectors and environmental influences, has provided a framework to embrace multiple and complex developmental characteristics. He has sought to envision the student as a total person engaged in an educational process that can significantly influence development; these processes range from classroom experiences to resident hall interactions. The breadth of his framework provides a panoramic view of complex variables without resort to reductionism.

The developmental vectors, however, do not all seem to be on the same plane. Some appear to be tasks, others are more similar to outcomes; in other words, some are processes and others are achievements. "Developing competence," "managing the emotions," and "freeing interpersonal relationships" are processes or tasks, but "becoming autonomous" or "establishing identity" are achievements that may occur as one gains skill in the processes. Establishing identity and becoming autonomous are not entirely completed at any stage of development; the other vectors would appear to be instrumental to them.

Is the term "integrity" a felicitous one for describing value development? It is misleading should the reader associate it with a character trait

---

[6]*Ibid.*, ch. 11.
[7]*Ibid.*, pp. 241–252.

approach in which integrity is only one of many different character traits identified but not sufficient to embrace them all. For instance, such an approach, in addition to integrity, may talk about such traits as honesty, loyalty, reliability, self-control, conscientiousness, benevolence, and the like.

Evidently what Chickering means is that integrity refers to the ability to organize values into internally consistent patterns to guide action, and the development of congruence between espoused values and conduct. This is an important aspect of value development but not the only important one. Other important abilities are the capacities to think through one's values, to analyze and critically appraise them so that they may be either reformulated or else, if accepted largely unchanged, one could provide adequate grounds for doing so.

Perhaps part of the problem lies in Chickering's definition of values: "Values are standards by which behavior is evaluated."[8] Standards, however, are only one among several types of value expression; moreover, values are not restricted in their functions to evaluating behavior. Value statements also take the form of rules (e.g., "Persons who smoke or drink will be denied membership.") and principles (the Golden Rule, which is actually a principle, and Kant's categorical imperative, one version of which says to "So act that the maxim of your will could always hold at the same time as a principle establishing universal law."). Values are also used to develop normative ethical systems (Epicureanism, Stoicism, Christian ethics, Kantian ethics, Utilitarianism).

Values are not limited to the evaluation of behavior, as they are integral to aesthetics and also take the form of utility values. Thus values are used to appraise a work of art (e.g., symmetry, harmony, color, texture, design, expressiveness, etc.). Utility values are used to appraise consumer products such as a new car (mileage per gallon, resale value, warranty, initial costs, spaciousness, etc.).

Chickering holds that "The proper function of colleges is to increase the role of values in the lives of students—not to modify the content of values held."[9] But certainly this claim cannot be made for church-related colleges that enroll irreligious students. Moreover, the claim seems inconsistent with Chickering's own position that colleges should develop salient, consistent institutional objectives that pervade college

---

[8]*Ibid.,* p. 123.

[9]*Ibid.,* p. 226.

life and are taken seriously by both faculty and students. Different patterns of institutional objectives can be discerned in some colleges.[10] What happens to a student, for instance, who comes from a home where he was taught to accept values on faith or authority and matriculates at a college that has as one of its objectives the promotion of critical thinking in all aspects of life? Obviously something will have to change in the student's value system if the college's faculty and students take institutional objectives seriously. Thus, Chickering's views notwithstanding, where institutional objectives are seriously pursued and a distinctive ambience and esprit de corps animates the college, value change will occur. As noted earlier in the Feldman and Newcomb review of research studies, value change does occur and it often persists after graduation.

PERRY AND HEATH:
GROWTH, COMMITMENT, AND MATURITY

Perry's longitudinal study of value development during the college years shows students moving from an early belief in authority's omniscience to relativism and finally to commitment, except for those students who suspend or reverse the process of growth.[11] Although his data are limited to the college setting and a single college (Harvard College), he believes it has wider implications for understanding late adolescence in a pluralistic society. By reviewing examination questions in large sections of freshman courses at Harvard College from 1900 to 1960, a shift can be discerned from seeking information and correct answers to a relativist stance, which was defined as considering questions in more than one frame of reference. In addition, Harvard has become increasingly diverse in its student body: 45 percent of its students in 1900 came from outside Massachusetts; in 1960, 72 percent. The significance of these changes is that students will confront a more relativistic, pluralistic environment that may seriously challenge their entering values.

A *Checklist of Educational Views* (CLEV) was devised to identify students in terms of certain desired dimensions; the CLEV was then administered to a random sample of 313 freshmen and, on the basis of

---

[10]*Ibid.*, ch. 8.

[11]Perry, William G.: *Forms of Intellectual and Ethical Development in the College Years: A Scheme.* New York, Holt, Rinehart and Winston, 1970.

their scores, invitations were sent to 55 students, 31 of whom accepted. Tape-recorded interviews were made in May and June each year, including 17 complete four-year records. Later the study was extended to obtain a larger sample of students' report of their four years in college, to articulate a developmental scheme found in the reports, and to test the scheme's validity. The researchers were able to show that the scheme of development could be identified in all the students' reports sampled.[12] In the study a *developmental pattern* was conceived as "an orderly progress in which more complex forms are created by the differentiation and reintegration of earlier, simple forms," and *growth* was defined simply as "progress in development."[13]

Perry observed three major value development stages: the modifying of dualism; the realizing of relativism; and the evolving of commitments. The line of development is in the order listed (dualism the early stage and commitments as the final stage). In each stage three positions were observed, consisting of a total of nine.

In terms of the dualistic stage, the child views his family and the outside world in position 1 according to in-group vs. outgroup. Morality consists of obedience to authority, with authority sometimes considered omniscient. Educational tasks are conceived in terms of memorization and hard work. Only three or four freshmen in the study were found at this position.

In Position 2 the student revolts against heterogeneity and, consequently, rejects critical thinking. Diversity and complexity are viewed as alien to him. But in Position 3 uncertainty and complexity are not considered obstacles generated by authority but existing independently. Here the student begins to question hard work in class as a basis for standards.

Positions 4 through 6 mark the emergence of relativism. The student perceives authority, in Position 4, as wanting him to think relativistically; he is still tied to what he believes authority wants him to do. By the time the student has reached Position 5, the dualistic structure of authority and the outside world has collapsed and knowledge is increasingly viewed as contextual and relativistic. This change comes about when it is seen that dualism cannot assimilate relativism. The student, in Position 6, apprehends the need for personal choice in a relativistic

---

[12]*Ibid.,* ch. 1.

[13]*Ibid.,* p. 44.

world; commitment is now viewed as the resolution of relativism, but it has yet to be experienced.

The last three positions move the student into the stage of commitment. Position 7 describes the student who has decided on his responsibility in some major area of his life, as in strongly stating a career decision. In Position 8 the student has developed a style for pursuing his commitment; finally, a person develops a sense of "who he is," both in content and style, in Position 9.

For Perry, growth is a moral issue insofar as the individual exhibits will, effort, and courage. A person who has moved to one of the higher positions is a "better" person. Courage is involved because one is faced with redefining and extending responsibilities in confronting increased uncertainty and complexity.

Perry claims that his study holds assumptions found in contextualistic pragmatism, post-Wittgensteinian Forms of Life, and existentialism as it refers to personal commitment. But it is not self-evident that such influences undergird the study unless the reader is first apprised of them and told to search for them.

Perry generalizes to other student populations from his limited sample. He also assumes that development from dualism to relativism to commitment is an advancement both intellectually and morally. Though it is obvious that the dualistic position has irremediable weaknesses, the weaknesses of the other stages are generally overlooked by Perry. Value relativism is unable to explain how one can show that another value position is wrong, as those values, which may be in opposition to one's own, may relate to a different context and social conditions. For instance, though a relativist may disapprove of infanticide, in a different culture that accepts the practice because of high birth rates, insufficient food, and the like, the relativist cannot say that this practice in the other culture is wrong.

Despite these misgivings, Perry's study has shown distinctly how development continues during the college years, the characteristic changes in development, and the way that these changes affect the thought and values of undergraduates. Teachers who use this schema to identify their students' stage of development could reshape their instruction to coincide with the students' present stage in order to communicate and evaluate more effectively.

A different approach to student development in college was pursued by Douglas Heath through the concept of maturity.[14] The first study's themes are What is a mature person? and How does a mature person adapt to disturbing information? The mature person, he found, manifests five traits: increases stability of organization so that one's identity can be maintained over time, seeks new information which is then made congruent with his self-organization, becomes progressively organized by internalizing social reality (allocentric) rather than need-dominated (autocentric), able increasingly to symbolically represent and coordinate more of his external and internal worlds, and becomes more autonomous for his decisions and actions.

The self, he claims, is composed of schemata, skills and valuators. The schema is a structure of internal psychic elements; the skill is an ability to cope with the environment; and the valuator consists of beliefs, interests, and preferences that serve as a basis of judgment and action.

Three samples were evaluated on a number of psychological measures (including Rorschach and MMPI). A panel of 18 judges (including nine students as well as faculty members) rated 24 Haverford upperclassmen. On several tests better organized students were able to analyze, conceptualize, and judge disturbing information more accurately and efficiently. The ability to recover from the disturbing information and to perform adaptively was positively related to MMPI Ego-strength scale.

His second book reports research studies over a ten-year period with various groups of Haverford College students: freshmen, sophomores, seniors, recent graduates, and other alumni. A number of research techniques were employed: standardized psychological tests, Self-image Questionnaire and the Perceived Self-questionnaire developed by Heath, and recorded standardized interviews.

Heath, once again, sought to assess changes in Haverford students in terms of what it means to mature (maturity is defined in terms of the characteristics stated above.) He notes four structures that define the person: intellectual growth, establishment of guiding values, increasing knowledge about oneself, and the development of social and interpersonal skills. By combining these four structures with the five characteristics of maturity generates 20 hypotheses concerning how a person grows.

---

[14]Heath, Douglas H., with the assistance of Heath, Harriet E.: *Explorations of Maturity: Studies of Mature and Immature College Men.* New York, Appleton-Century-Crofts, 1965; and Heath, Douglas H.: *Growing Up In College: Liberal Education and Maturity.* San Francisco, Jossey-Bass, 1968.

The investigation involved 73 randomly selected subjects; comparisons with nonparticipants in the study showed few differences. Analysis of the data provided a large number of statistically significant correlations. In terms of the principal developmental changes, the seniors were more mature than freshmen and may have matured beyond where they themselves were as freshmen. The rate of maturing varied in different sectors of the personality. Maturing in autonomy and in personal relations was more frequently discerned than in symbolization.

Heath also evaluated alumni and found somewhat different effects of college than from students presently enrolled. Maturing of one's values became more significant for alumni and one's interpersonal relations less significant. The maturing effects of college are a more stabilized, integrated self-concept.

In these studies Heath has sensitively observed changes in development, and he makes important contributions to our thinking about psychological health. His conceptual framework is able to formulate hypotheses with a high level of generality, and the studies skillfully integrate theoretical and empirical approaches.

Generalizations, however, must be limited from the Haverford student population because it is a small, highly selective residential college. Heath's personality variables are a set of assumptions rather than a theory, and more precisely stated hypotheses need to be drawn. He is actually studying psychological health rather than maturity, as the latter concept can more plausibly be defined in terms of assuming responsibility in appropriate social roles and adapting successfully to adult norms—traits which may not necessarily have a high correlation with psychological health. Though Heath has important ideas to convey, his presentation is frequently repetitious and diffuse. In dealing with students' ethical motives, he should have observed actual life crises. Finally, the studies need replication in a different setting by another researcher.

KENISTON: UNCOMMITTED AND DISSIDENT YOUTH

Kenneth Keniston has been a keen observer during the 1960s and early 1970s of uncommitted and dissident youth. In Keniston's study of the uncommitted, he takes up two themes: one theme is based on three years of research with uncommitted students at Harvard College; the other theme focuses on an analysis of the maladies and failures of technological society.[15] (Only the first theme will be discussed.)

In identifying uncommitted students, subjects were interviewed and given the Thematic Apperception Test. Symptoms of alienation discerned include pessimism, resentment, distrust, anxiety, egocentricity, sense of being an outsider, and rejection of happiness as a goal. Those scoring high on indices were classified as alienated; low, classified as conformists; and another group of 12 were classified as "extremely non-alienated," and those of average classification as "not extreme either way."

Alienated youth studied were passionately interested in intellectual and aesthetic activities, enjoyed verbal disputes, professed agnosticism, and evinced a distrust of human nature and all ideologies. These young men rejected conventional American values, especially occupational and family roles. Instead they restlessly searched for adventure and new experiences; they have a rich fantasy life and yearn for fusion or loss of selfhood. They were too alienated to become beatniks (which involves accepting an identity, some solidarity) and were not politically active.

Their characteristics, as uncovered by Keniston in intensive clinical interviews with 12 Harvard men, were an identification with their mothers, who were described as highly sensitive, frustrated, aesthetic women; while their fathers depicted their sons as having failed to realize their fathers' aspirations for them. These youth also evinced a revulsion toward the values of conventional youth culture and the educational system. The major themes in their lives, says Keniston, are but extreme reactions that affect all youth.

Keniston has illuminated the lives of uncommitted youth. He does not present in any detail, however, the methodology which generated the data. The reader also is not given a portrait of the two other control groups. Specific alienation problems were combined rather than separated (e.g., alienation of youth, alienation of intellectuals, alienation based on marginal psychological characteristics and traumas).

Keniston's study of radical youth involved interviews with 17 youths who participated in "Vietnam Summer," a movement in opposition to America's activities in Southeast Asia.[16] This is a study in political socialization.

---

[15]Keniston, Kenneth: *The Uncommitted: Alienated Youth in American Society.* New York, Harcourt, Brace & World, 1965.

[16]Keniston, Kenneth: *Young Radicals: Notes on Committed Youth.* New York: Harcourt, Brace, & World, 1968.

These youths came from affluent homes where parents treated them with directness and humanity; parents permitted their views to be criticized. But they still identified with parents selectively by imitating those qualities they perceived as valuable and opposing other qualities. The young radicals retained a set of core values concerning relationships, motives, and feelings but rejected the political philosophies and institutions that systematized them.

Keniston found previous explanations inadequate: the young radical was neither a "radical rebel" (a rejection of authority derived from rejection of authority of one's family) nor a "red-diaper baby" (radicalism learned from one's radical parents).

Instead he postulates the "stage of youth," a stage that intervenes between adolescence and adulthood that arose as society freed youth from the need to work while concurrently demanding more formal education. Keniston does not regard his subjects' radicalism as a neurotic defense mechanism but as a natural and integrated part of their life experiences.

Postmodern youth may not face in their parents a gap between preaching and practice any greater than previous generations; yet because of rapid social changes and parental ambivalence between early values of their own childhood and those of their adulthood, they are unable to rationalize the discrepancy between creed and deed. Today's youth, therefore, may be able to perceive this discrepancy better than earlier youth.

Keniston has also brought together 20 essays; all but two have been published before.[17] Some essays seem fragmentary and incomplete; his earlier essays, which contain typologies later abandoned, lead the reader to question why he included these selections. This dichotomy between uncommitted and radicals forces many different youth styles into these categories even though most youth do not fit into either one. Keniston's studies do not include women and nonwhites; he especially overlooked a significant opportunity to study the black protest movement of the 1960s.

Despite these misgivings, his studies have traced dissent from the Civil Rights sit-ins and the Berkeley Free Speech movement. Keniston perceives the youth rebellion as international in scope, a combination of a new psychological stage and peculiar historical conditions. Thus he

---

[17]Keniston, Kenneth: *Youth and Dissent: The Rise of a New Opposition.* New York, Harcourt Brace Jovanovich, 1971.

finds that the college experience promotes more complex, individuated persons whose presence in a confused and rapidly changing society stimulates the emergence of countercultures.

In summary, it has been shown that many fruitful theories of moral development in the undergraduate years have advanced our understanding and laid to rest the findings of the Jacob study; thus the college experience can have a significant influence on moral and personal development and bring about value change. These changes continue after college according to Douglas Heath's study of 68 male college graduates in their thirties who had become more mature on all of the general measures of maturity used in the study.[18] Thus, as Withey observed, college may be the last important opportunity for a self-confronting experience. "It provides an opportunity of meeting people of varying backgrounds with different ideas, at a time of life when self-examination is maximized and in an institution that legitimizes the identity task of exploring and reevaluating one's values and ideologies."[19]

---

[18]Heath, Dougleas R.: What the enduring effects of higher education tell us about a liberal education. *Journal of Higher Education,* 47:173–190, March–April, 1976.

[19]Withey, S.B.: *A Degree and What Else? Correlates and Consequences of a College Education.* New York, McGraw-Hill, 1971, p. 39.

Chapter 5

MORAL DEVELOPMENT
THROUGH THE LIFE SPAN

KOHLBERG: COGNITIVE
MORAL DEVELOPMENT THEORY

LAWRENCE Kohlberg and his associates have conducted research over the past several decades on a cognitive moral development theory, and the theory has been an object of considerable attention and debate within the international academic community. His theory was influenced by Dewey's psychological writings,[1] and also is indebted to Piaget's pioneering work.[2]

Kohlberg has sought to overcome the deficiencies of Piaget's research by using a much larger sample that is more broadly based socially and is composed of equal proportions of popular and socially isolated children. He is also concerned with the principle of justice rather than, as with Piaget, simple virtues and vices and such concepts as cooperation and equity.

Rather than relative values, Kohlberg's findings show culturally universal stages of moral development. His theory, he claims, is both psychological and philosophical, and his findings generate a philosophy of moral education designed to stimulate moral development rather than teach fixed moral rules. Kohlberg believes that a philosophic concept of morality and moral development is required, that moral development passes through invariant qualitative stages, and that moral development is stimulated by promoting thinking and problem-solving.

Kohlberg's study yielded six developmental stages allotted to three

---

[1]However, Kohlberg's universal ethical values, along with other aspects of his theory, differ from Dewey's views, which are transactional and situational.

[2]For Kohlberg's early development of his theory, along with his criticisms of Piaget, see his: Development of moral character and moral ideology. In Hoffman, M.L. and Hoffman, L.W. (Eds.): *Review of Child Development Research.* New York, Russell Sage Foundation, 1964, vol. I, pp. 383–431; Stage and sequence: The cognitive development approach to socialization. In Goslin, D.A. (Ed.): *Handbook of Socialization Theory and Research,* Chicago, Rand McNally, 1969, pp. 347–480.

moral levels. Subsequent retesting of the groups at three-year intervals has shown growth proceeding through the same stages in the same order.

I.   *Preconventional Level*

    Stage 1:   Orientation to punishment, obedience, and physical and material power. Rules are obeyed to avoid punishment.

    Stage 2:   Naive instrumental hedonistic orientation. The child conforms to obtain rewards.

II. *Conventional Level*

    Stage 3:   "Good boy" orientation designed to win approval and maintain expectations of one's immediate group. The child conforms to avoid disapproval. One earns approval by being "nice."

    Stage 4:   Orientation to authority, law, and duty, to maintain a fixed order, whether social or religious. Right behavior consists of doing one's duty and abiding by the social order.

III. *Postconventional, Autonomous, or Principled Level*

    Stage 5:   Social contract orientation, in which duties are defined in terms contract and the respect of others' rights. Emphasis is upon equality and mutual obligation within a democratic order. There is an awareness of relativism of personal values and the use of procedural rules in reaching consensus.

    Stage 6:   The morality of individual principles of conscience that have logical comprehensiveness and universality. Rightness of acts is determined by conscience in accord with ethical principles that appeal to comprehensiveness, universality, and consistency. These principles are not concrete (like the Ten Commandments) but general and abstract (like the Golden Rule, the categorical imperative).

These stages are based on ways of thinking about moral matters. Stages 1 and 2 are characteristic of young children; whereas Stages 3 and 4, according to Kohlberg, are ones at which most of the adult population operates. No more than 20 to 25 percent of the adult population have reached the last two stages, with only about 5 to 10 percent at Stage 6.

However, after failing to find Stage 6 subjects in Turkey, Kohlberg reduced the number of stages to five by making Stage 6 an advanced

Stage 5 form.[3] Kohlberg also postulated the existence of a Stage 7 that involves contemplative experience of a nonegoistic and nondualistic variety.[4] But since no empirical evidence of this stage has been found, and since Stage 6 has been abandoned, Stage 7 can also be discarded from his theory.

Kohlberg insists that schools have been teaching a "bag of virtues"—a particular set of values and character traits that are culturally relative.[5] These virtues range from Aristotle's choice of temperance, liberality, pride, good temper, truthfulness, and justice to the well known Boy Scout bag. These and other virtues are instilled by exhortation, example, and practice.

In his objection to the bag of virtues approach, Kohlberg cites the landmark Character Education Inquiry in the 1920s.[6] The vast majority of pupils, on the basis of tests administered, acted honestly in some situations and dishonestly in others, and there was consistency in these patterns when the tests were repeated. It was concluded that behavior is highly specific, depending upon the particular case; there is no such thing as honest and dishonest children but only honest and dishonest acts. Thus little evidence was found of unified character traits or generality in moral behavior.

Kohlberg offers several other objections to this approach.[7] Arbitrariness exists in composing the list of virtues, depending upon the composition of committees to develop such a list, their agreements and inconsistencies. Virtue words are relative to cultural standards that are psychologically vague and ethically relative (e.g., the inability to agree on the meaning of "self-discipline"). Moreover, by labeling a set of behaviors with a positive or negative trait does not in itself show that it is of ethical importance but represents an appeal to social conventions. Additionally, longitudinal research findings raise doubts whether child-

---

[3]Kohlberg, Lawrence: Revisions in the theory and practice of moral development. In Damon, William (Ed.): *Moral Development.* San Francisco: Jossey-Bass, 1978, pp. 83–87.

[4]Kohlberg, Lawrence: Stages and aging in moral development—some speculations. *The Gerontologist,* 13:497–502, 1973.

[5]Kohlberg, Lawrence: Education for justice: A modern statement of the Platonic view. In Sizer, Theodore R. and Sizer, Nancy F.: *Moral Education: Five Lectures.* Cambridge, Mass., Harvard University Press, 1970.

[6]Hartshorne, Hugh and May, M.A.: *Studies in the Nature of Character: Studies in Deceit* (Vol. I), Studies in Service and Self-Control (Vol. II), Studies in Organization of Character (Vol. III). New York, Macmillan, 1928–30.

[7]Kohlberg, Lawrence: Development as the aim of education: The Dewey view. *Harvard Educational Review,* 42, no. 4:449–496, 1972.

hood personality traits are stable or predictive over time and stages of development. Childhood traits, as used in Head Start, are not predictive of positive or negative adjustment. Research suggests that various character traits do not stand for consistent personality traits but are merely evaluative labels.[8]

Returning to the stages of development, Kohlberg contends that the stages are "structured wholes," or organized systems of thought. Stages imply qualitatively different modes of thinking. Second, stages form an invariant sequence. Third, stages are "hierarchical integrations."[9]

Stages are defined according to responses to moral dilemmas classified in terms of a scoring scheme. Validating studies include a twenty-five year study of fifty Chicago-area boys, middle and working class; a six-year study of Turkish village and city boys of the same age; and various cross-sectional studies in Britain, Canada, India, Israel, Honduras, Taiwan, and Yucatan.

Stages are organized systems of thought, as about 67 percent of most subjects' thinking is at a single stage irrespective of which moral dilemma is used to test it. The typology is referred to as "stages" because they represent invariant developmental sequences: all movement is forward and does not omit steps, the stages arise one at a time and in the same order, even though children move through the stages at varying speeds. The stages are hierarchical insofar as thinking at a higher stage comprehends within it thinking at lower stages. Individuals prefer the highest stage available to them in their thinking because higher stages can more adequately organize the multiplicity of data, interests, and possibilities open to each person. Thus the higher stages are not only more socially adaptive but are philosophically superior because they move the individual closer to basing moral decisions upon a concept of justice (Stage 6). This is the level of principles which can be universalized (i.e., applied to all persons everywhere), where the individual views moral judgment not from his or her individual perspective or society's values, but from the perspective of any human being. Thus, following Kant, Stage 6 universalizes moral principles.

Both Kohlberg and Piaget are structuralists. Kohlberg states that Piaget's theory is *structured* because it abstracts a form of thinking or structure

---

[8]Kohlberg: Education for justice, pp. 69–70.

[9]Kohlberg: Stage and sequence.

from the *function* which the thinking is serving.[10] The same function (moral judgment) is served by successive structures of judgment which displace or reintegrate prior structures for serving this purpose. In contrast, Kohlberg claims that Erikson's theory is functional because it defines stages not by structures but by new functions of the self, person, or ego.

In keeping with the structuralism of Kohlberg's theory, the moral stages are considered *structures* of moral judgment as opposed to the *content* of moral judgment. As an example, in one of the moral dilemmas an issue is raised whether the husband of a dying woman should steal a drug if the seller refuses to reduce his price and the husband cannot raise the money to afford to purchase it. Whether or not to steal the drug is the content of the moral judgment in the situation; reasoning about the choice defines the structure of the moral judgment. The individual's structure of moral judgment is embodied in what he or she defines as valuable in the moral issues raised, and the reasons given for holding the value(s). Thus in Stage 1, for instance, life is valued for power or possessions; whereas only in Stages 5 and 6 is life viewed as inherently worthwhile, apart from other considerations.

Since the stages relate to the structure of moral judgment, it might be inferred that anyone who can reason logically would be rated at one of the more advanced stages; yet such ratings would be fallacious because a person could use logical reasoning effectively but still not act morally. Kohlberg claims that advanced moral reasoning depends upon logical reasoning—it is necessary for moral development and sets limits to it; however, most individuals are higher in logical stage than moral stage.

Kohlberg has recognized, in light of certain philosophical criticisms of his theory, that an adequate psychological theory that explains why a person moves from one stage to the next needs an adequate philosophical explanation as to why a higher stage is more adequate than a lower stage.[11] Such developments are different than the learning of cultural roles and systems of thought based on cultural or ethical relative views. Relativism can be classified into three types: *descriptive relativism* holds that basic ethical beliefs of different people and societies are divergent

---

[10]Kohlberg, Lawrence: Continuities in childhood and adult moral development revisited. In Baltes, P. and Schaie, K.W. (Eds.): *Life-span Developmental Psychology.* New York, Academic Press, 1973.

[11]Kohlberg, Lawrence: From *is* to *ought:* How to commit the naturalistic fallacy and get away with it in the study of moral development. In *The Philosophy of Moral Development: Moral Stages and the Idea of Justice.* New York, Harper & Row, 1981, pp. 101–189.

and conflicting; *normative relativism* states that what is right and good for
one individual or society is not right or good for another; and *meta-
ethical relativism* holds that there is no valid or rational way of justifying
one set of ethical judgments against another.[12]

Kohlberg cites illustrations from psychoanalysis, anthropology, and
other fields to show the problems of relativism (though Kohlberg lumps
normative and meta-ethical relativism under the rubric "ethical relativism"). One example is where a patient asks his analyst why his striving
for power is inauthentic and bad; he is then told that it is based on
anxiety; and when the patient wants to know why that makes it bad, the
psychoanalyst says that such terms cannot be logically analyzed—only
scientific ones are subject to such analysis. Another example is anthropologists' confusion of cultural tolerance with cultural relativism by
trying to show that no principles are universalizable; consequently, the
values of white imperialistic nations were not better than those native
people that they ruled. A third fallacy is to confuse scientific thinking in
the social sciences with value neutralism. But value "neutrality" is not
neutral because it prejudges the facts by assuming that there are no
culturally universal values.

A more moderate brand of relativism, sociological relativism, holds
that moral terms and judgments are used in all cultures, while the
content of morality varies according to the culture. Kohlberg, in response,
contends that there is less variation in cultures than is usually imagined
because all cultures use basic moral categories, concepts, or principles;
and all individuals, whatever the culture, go through the same sequence
of moral development. But, one may ask, why does such great moral
diversity exist among cultures? Kohlberg's explanation is that the differences lie in the stage of moral development of individuals and cultures
and in the meaning, use, and hierarchical ordering of value concepts.
These cultural divergencies are not only found in the knowledge base
but in the principles used in moral evaluations. Nevertheless, the stages
of moral development, Kohlberg concludes, are culturally universal,
occur in an invariant developmental order, and the interpretations of the
categories are universal.[13]

The claim that the higher stage's mode of judgment is more adequate
than a lower stage is based on the conditions of morality rather than

---

[12]Frankena, William K.: *Ethics,* 2nd ed. Englewood Cliffs, N.J., Prentice-Hall, 1973, p. 109.

[13]Kohlberg: From *is* to *ought.*

rationality or some other external factor. Kohlberg means that morality is a unique realm that has distinctive formal characteristics in formulating moral judgments: impersonality, universalizability, ideality, preemptiveness, and other features. In other words, moral reasons have these characteristics. Thus this is part of his theory's formalism—its emphasis on the form of moral judgment rather than the content.

Kohlberg admits that he is committing one form of the naturalistic fallacy: asserting that what moral judgment ought to be should rest on an adequate conception of what it actually is. (It is considered a fallacy when ethical statements are reduced to factual statements, or when ethical statements are derived from factual statements.) What he actually claims is that it has been shown scientifically that there are universal moral forms centering on the principle of justice; science, therefore, can determine whether a philosopher's conception of morality accords with psychological facts; in turn, normative ethical analysis can show whether a particular moral philosophy can or cannot effectively handle certain moral problems that such analysis has previously delineated. Although psychological and normative analysis cannot be reduced to one another, the two are parallel or isomorphic and, consequently, the psychological descriptions of moral stages correspond to the deeper structure of normative ethics.

Assessment of the Cognitive Moral Development Theory

The cognitive moral development theory has attracted scholarly attention internationally and numerous critics and supporters have emerged. First, some criticisms of the theory are offered before drawing upon supporting evidence.

Some criticisms are directed toward the developmental stages and the logical order in the stages themselves.[14] The stages need to be delineated more precisely: the distinction between Stages 5 and 6 is not clear; conceptual links can be found between Stages 2 and 5 that do not exist between 2 and 3; and possibly more advanced stages are needed as well as finer calibration within the stages. It has also been suggested that the stages lack any necessary connection with moral action and therefore what has been provided are stages of general cognitive, rather than

---

[14]Beck, C.M. and Others (Eds.): *Moral education: Interdisciplinary approaches.* Toronto, University of Toronto Press, 1971, pp. 355–72.

moral, development. Williams and Williams, on the basis of their data, believe that Stages 3 and 4 are parallel or alternate rather than sequential developmental steps.[15]

That individuals move through these stages in an invariant sequence is disputed by Simpson, who contends that this has only been demonstrated for Stages 2, 3, and 4. She claims that the stages are not culturally universal, because Kohlberg has not studied a sufficient number of cultures to substantiate the claims, and he did not find postconventional reasoning in all the cultures studied. If postconventional reasoning is more prevalent in urban cultures that are Western influenced, then Kohlberg's higher stages are culturally biased.[16]

Kohlberg has responded to Simpson's charges.[17] He admits that Stage 5 reasoning shows a low frequency in Western and non-Western cultures; yet Stage 5 has been found in a fairly large number of such cultures. That Stage 5 recurs with low frequency has no logical bearing on the claim that Stage 5 exists as a structure. The pertinent question in this context is to identify the socioenvironmental conditions that impede or facilitate the emergence of principled reasoning.

Part of Simpson's argument is that the method of assessing competence is linguistically dependent. Kohlberg replies that studies conducted in the U.S. show a low to moderate correlation between verbal fluency or complexity and moral stage. Studies in Israel and Turkey since Simpson's critique found invariance in stages among the college educated. Such stages, however, have not been observed in urban villages, most likely because their social structure is relatively simple and they have little or no formal education.

Kohlberg answers Simpson's charge of cultural bias of rating one culture as having more moral worth than another by observing that there is no way that group averages can be translated into relative moral worth of groups. A judgment of a particular practice (e.g., Aztec's human sacrifice) does not constitute a moral evaluation of a culture. Moreover, a person who scores at Stage 5 can resolve more moral problems than one at Stage 3; yet it is not a claim that the former has more moral worth than the latter.

---

[15]Williams, N. and Williams, S.: *The Moral Development of Children.* London, Macmillan, 1970.

[16]Simpson, Elizabeth L.: Moral development research: A case study of scientific cultural bias. *Human Development,* 17:81–106, 1974.

[17]Kohlberg, Lawrence: *The Psychology of Moral Development* (San Francisco: Harper & Row, 1984), ch. 4.

Simpson claims that Kohlberg's theory is part of the interaction of his personality with a specifiable social environment. Kohlberg accuses her of committing the genetic fallacy. The genetic fallacy involves arguing that the origin of something is identical with that from which it originates. To avoid bias in theory development is not to be a relativist but to use the scientific method and critical appraisal. Fraenkel observes a contradiction in stage formulation: if the higher stages are better, they should contain something not found in the lower stages; yet if this is the case, how will those at the lower stages understand the arguments of those at the higher stages and accept such reasoning as better than their own? But if higher is not better, there seems to be no justification for helping the young to move through the stages.[18]

Kohlberg's criticism of the "bag of virtues" approach comes under scrutiny by Peters.[19] He considers it strange to contrast a morality of principles with a morality of character traits. Being just or fair are paradigm cases of character traits; to call something a character trait—such as honesty or justness—is to suggest that someone has made a rule of his own. He adds that Kohlberg's criticism of character traits rests largely on the peculiar features of honesty as a character trait. Dishonesty has to be understood in terms of such specific situations as lying, cheating, and fraud; other virtues and vices—benevolence, cruelty, and integrity—are not ties to specific types of action. Since young children cannot grasp a principled morality (the higher stages), he recommends that they learn good habits in an intelligent way as a basis for a later period when they can determine grounds for accepting or rejecting rules. Virtues of self-control and moral courage need to be developed not only because of their value in the child's life but for their ability to sustain the individual later at the principled level so as to be able to act on principle without great stress and guilt.

Rich contends that the primary problem of Kohlberg's approach to the emotions is his assumption that emotions are irrational or nonrational forces in conflict with the cognitive core of moral development instead of his developing a cognitive approach to the emotions in relation to moral

---

[18]Fraenkel, Jack R.: The Kohlberg bandwagon: Some reservations. In Purpel, D. and Ryan, K. (Eds.): *Moral Education: It Comes with the Territory.* Berkeley, McCutchan, 1976, pp. 291–307.

[19]Peters, R.S.: Moral development: A plea for pluralism. In his *Psychology and Ethical Development.* London, Allen & Unwin, 1974, pp. 303–335.

judgment.[20] It is claimed that to relate the cognitive developmental theory to the emotions, some use must be made of character traits. Suggestive of this reconciliation is the use of Kohlberg's treatment of motives for engaging in moral action. The character traits could therefore become patterned behavioral counterparts of the respective underlying principles in the Conventional and Postconventional levels. As examples, conscientiousness would be a primary trait at the Conventional level; compassion, benevolence, and fairness at the Postconventional level.

Gilligan notes that Kohlberg found women, in light of their strong interpersonal orientation, to favor Stage 3, a stage he held to be functional and adequate for them. She laments that the traits that have conventionally defined the "goodness" of women—their care and sensitivity to the needs of others—are those that mark them as deficient in moral development. She suggests that Kohlberg's scoring system may be biased against women because of the disproportionate number of males in research samples and that the developmental theories themselves tend to be formulated by men.[21]

In contrast to Freud and Piaget, Kohlberg says that he does not claim that females have a less developed sense of justice than males; rather, he holds that women would need opportunities in education and work for the necessary development of Stages 4 and 5 reasoning. In the "just community" approach in democratically resolving moral issues, conflicting rights are interwoven with caring and responsibility. At the hypothetical sixth stage, justice and care forms a single moral principle. Both sexes used justice and responsibility considerations in school dilemmas. The major differences in the two orientations were the type of dilemma asked and the sociomoral atmosphere of the school situation. It remains for Gilligan to demonstrate that there are "hard" stages (in the Piagetian sense of stage) in the care orientation.[22]

Other criticisms relate to the measurement instruments employed. Kurtines and Grief question the empirical validity of the theory's basic premises because of the complexity of administering and scoring the instruments, lack of standardization in administering the tests, and the

---

[20]Rich, John Martin: Morality, reason and emotions. In Modgil, S. and Modgil, C. (Eds.): *Lawrence Kohlberg: Consensus and Controversy.* Sussex, England, Falmer Press, 1986, pp. 209–219.

[21]Gilligan, Carol: In a different voice: Women's conception of self and morality. *Harvard Educational Review,* 47:43–59, 1977.

[22]Kohlberg: *Psychology of Moral Development,* ch. 4.

high chance of rater bias in scoring.[23] Broughton has responded to these criticisms and sought to defend the theory against these charges.[24] Carroll and Rest indicate that the scoring system has been developed over 20 years and, in contrast to Piaget's nine dimensions, it identifies hundreds of features.[25] The system uses longitudinal as well as cross-sectional data, provides ways for handling free-response interview material, and supplies an analytical scheme for classifying the thinking of moral philosophers.

Other studies also support the theory. Do children skip stages or move through them in mixed-up order? Kuhn tested younger children at six-month intervals and found orderly progression with no evidence of skipping.[26] Kohlberg has recently completed a 20-year longitudinal study that found no skipping, with gradual change in all subjects.[27]

If the developmental stage view is correct, Turiel reports, then children should be responsible to influences that attempt to direct them to the next higher stage.[28] He employed role-playing in which children age 12 to 13½ were exposed to moral reasoning at their own stage and at other stages. Children showed more of a tendency to be influenced by arguments one stage above their own than one stage below.

Rest has shown that moral judgments cannot be simply equated with verbal facility or general cognitive development, as measures of moral thinking are more closely correlated among themselves than with general cognitive ability.[29] He has also found that subjects are not 100 percent in one or another stage and, consequently, development involves gradual shifts rather than a step-by-step progression.[30]

Kohlberg has recently altered his position about moral education by

---

[23]Kurtines, William and Grief, Esther B.: The development of moral thought: Review and evaluation of Kohlberg's work. *Psychological Bulletin*, 81:453–70, 1974.

[24]Broughton, John: The cognitive-developmental approach to morality. *Journal of Moral Education*, 7:81–96, January, 1978.

[25]Carroll, James L. and Rest, James R.: Moral development. In Wolman, Benjamin B. (Ed.): *Handbook of Developmental Psychology*. Englewood Cliffs, N.J.: Prentice-Hall, 1982, pp. 434–451.

[26]Kuhn, D.: Short-term longitudinal evidence for the sequentiality of Kohlberg's early stages of moral judgment. *Developmental Psychology*, 12:162–166, 1976.

[27]Kohlberg, Lawrence: *The Meaning and Measurement of Moral Development.* Clark Lectures, Clark University, 1979.

[28]Turiel, E.: Developmental processes in the child's moral thinking. In Mussen, P.H. et al. (Eds.): *Trends and Issues in Developmental Psychology.* New York, Holt, 1969, pp. 92–133.

[29]Rest, J.R.: *Development in Judging Moral Issues.* Minneapolis: University of Minnesota Press, 1979.

[30]*Ibid.,* ch. 3.

claiming that such education must be partly "indoctrinative" because one cannot wait until children reach the fifth stage before dealing directly with their moral behavior.[31] The teacher, he believes, can indoctrinate or advocate without violating children's rights so long as students participate in rule-making and the value upholding process.

Kohlberg's claims have been tested in a number of cross-cultural studies. Snarey reviewed 45 studies from 27 cultural groups and found considerable support of the invariance of the stage sequence, with the first two stages identified in a wide range of cultural settings. Postconventional moral reasoning seems to be limited to complex urban societies (both Western and non-Western), as no evidence has been found for postconventional stages in any of the eight "folk tribal or village societies" studied.[32]

Shweder and others, in terms of research in India, have proposed alternative postconventional moralities based upon conceptions of natural law and justice and possibly modeled on the family as a moral institution rather than individualism, secularism, and social contract.[33] Based on studies in Hong Kong, Ma has proposed a revised theory of moral development that would include Chinese perspectives such as the "Golden Mean" (behaving as the majority of people in society do) and "Good Will" (the virtue of complying with nature). Samples drawn from England, Hong Kong, and the People's Republic of China revealed a stronger tendency in the two Chinese samples for people to perform altruistic acts and abide by the law. Generally, the Chinese emphasize human affection more than reason, and they value filial piety, group solidarity and collectivism.[34] Thus, in light of these cross-cultural findings, a reconceptualization of postconventional morality is needed.

The educational applications of the theory have been to promote classroom discussion of moral issues to stimulate moral growth, and to restructure the school environment. An attempt is made in the discussion groups to arouse cognitive conflict among participants and expose them to moral reasoning of a stage higher than their own. No separate

---

[31]Kohlberg: Revisions in the theory and practice of moral development, pp. 84–85.

[32]Snarey, J.R.: Cross-cultural universality of social-moral development: A critical review of Kohlbergian research. *Psychological Bulletin*, 97:202–232, 1985.

[33]Shweder, R.A.; Mahapatra, M.; Miller, J.G. Culture and moral development. In Stigler, J.; Shweder, R.A.; Herdt, G. (Eds.): *Cultural Psychology*. New York: Cambridge University Press, 1990, pp. 130–204.

[34]Ma, H.K.: Moral orientation and moral judgments in adolescents in Hong Kong, Mainland China, and England. *Journal of Cross-Cultural Psychology*, 20: 152–177, 1989.

courses are proposed; rather, discussions of this type could take place in social studies, law education, philosophy and sex education.

Democratic governance, Kohlberg believes, is the basis of the "just community approach" whereby students learn to democratically share decision-making responsibility. One experiment along these lines is Cambridge alternative school which is run as a direct democracy. Although school rules are in effect, everyone participates in the right to interpret and enforce these rules in weekly meetings in which such decisions are made.

The first approach that raises moral issues to stimulate moral change is not a curriculum for moral education and has not been integrated into the larger curriculum. Insufficiently trained teachers in using this approach tend to misuse the stages by labelling their students. In the just community approach, students, by the second year, learned to take an active role in dealing with school problems.

In conclusion, Piaget's influence on Kohlberg's thinking was indicated, the advancements of Kohlberg's theory should be evident insofar as it has attempted to integrate (though not always successfully) philosophical, psychological, and pedagogical concerns. The theory has stimulated much research and criticism and thereby opened new ways of thinking about moral development.

LEVINSON: THE SEASONS OF ADULT LIFE CYCLES

Daniel Levinson and his associates conducted a longitudinal study of 40 men over a ten-year period using a multidisciplinary approach.[35] Recognizing that much more is known about childhood and adolescence than the adult years, the study acknowledged the pioneer work of Jung and Erikson in the exploration of adult development while seeking to create its own framework of analysis and methodology.

The concepts developed include "life cycle," "seasons," and "era." *Life cycle* suggests that life has a certain character and follows a basic sequence. Life has a starting point and a terminating point; it has an underlying, universal pattern even though many individual and cultural variations can be observed.

Seasons signify stages or periods within the life cycle. Seasons vary qualitatively and are not simple, continuous, and unchanging. A season

---

[35]Levinson, Daniel J., et al.: *The Seasons of a Man's Life.* New York: Knopf, 1978.

is a relatively stable part of the total cycle. Each season has its own internal time and no season is more important than any other one, as each contributes to the whole and is a part of the total cycle.

An *era* is a time of life that has distinctive and unifying qualities that are more inclusive than a developmental stage. The four eras are: childhood and adolescence, early adulthood, middle adulthood, and late adulthood. The study focuses on the late teens to the late forties.

The researchers decided to limit their study to men because the differences between the sexes are sufficiently great that to study 20 men and 20 women would not do justice to either group. Chosen for the study were four subgroups of 10 men between the ages of 35 and 45, selected from four occupational categories: hourly workers in industry, business executives, university biologists, and novelists. Occupations were chosen because of the assumptions that man's work is the primary basis for his life in society and for its source of fulfillment and frustration in shaping his self-concept.

The men chosen live between Boston and New York and are drawn from a diverse sample in terms of social class, racial-ethnic-religious origins, education, and marital status. Each man was seen five to ten times for a total of ten to twenty hours in two to three months, and, in most instances, follow-up interviews occurred two years after the initial interviews. "Biographical interviewing," a central methodological feature, attempted to construct a story of each man's life. In order to elicit personal experiences, the Thematic Apperception Test was used as part of interviewing and, as a biographical supplement, the researchers drew upon some biographies from famous persons in history and imaginary figures in fiction and drama.

An understanding during the era of middle adulthood may be enhanced by the concept of "individual life structure"—the underlying pattern of an individual's life at a given time. Such patterns are comprised of an individual's occupation, love relationships, marriage and family, various social relations, and relations with oneself. Life structure can be studied by examining the critical choices an individual makes and how he deals with the consequences. One or two components play a vital role in the structure, while others are peripheral. A man may put his occupation first and later start detaching himself from it and place his family in a more central position. Important components in men's lives are occupation, marriage-family, religion, ethnicity, friendships, and leisure (usually the first two are the most important ones).

The study focuses on two eras: early adulthood and middle adulthood, with each area divided into a number of seasons or periods. The stages of the former era are listed below:

Early Adulthood

Age range	Stage
17–22	Early Adult Transition
22–28	Entering Adult World
28–33	Age 30 Transition
33–40	Settling Down

The first three periods are spoken of by Levinson as "the novice phase" because entering adulthood is more complex and prolonged than commonly imagined and it therefore takes these three periods to complete the task. The two major tasks of the first period, the Early Adult Transition, are to leave the pre-adult world and take a preliminary step into the adult world. This means that the young person must separate from the family and from individuals and groups in the pre-adult world. Part of this separation and initiation into adulthood may come through experience in the armed forces or in college attendance.

One finding was that the great majority of men in the sample formed a life in early adulthood quite different from that of their parents. The significant differences lie in values and life style rather than income or social class. Many changed their religion or married a woman of another religion; some moved into a subculture that held different values from those of their parents.

It is commonly believed that a young man enters adulthood in his early twenties and, after a period of exploration, chooses a relatively stable path. In contrast, the study found that few men build their first adult structure without considerable difficulty and occasional crisis. The two tasks of the second period, Entering the Adult World, are exploration—to look at one's options and keep them open—and to create an initial adult life structure. For most men in the late twenties their life structure is unstable and fragmented: they may have had a series of jobs but no clear occupational direction.

The Age 30 Transition, the third period in early adulthood, offers an opportunity to overcome the weaknesses in the life structure formed during the previous period and to create a more satisfactory structure. For some men an age 30 crisis ensues.

The novice phase (the first three periods) has four major tasks: forming a Dream and providing it a place in the life structure; forming mentor relationships; forming an occupation; forming love relationships, marriage and family. Levinson found that the mentoring relationship is also situated in a work setting, the mentor is usually eight to fifteen years older than the protégé and the relationship lasts two or three years on the average. The mentor functions as a transitional figure and represents a mixture of parent and peer but not exclusively one. The mentor can serve one or more functions: teacher, sponsor, host and guide, or counselor. The most crucial function is that the mentor facilitate "the realization of the Dream." The "dream" is initially a vague vision, poorly articulated to reality, of what the person would like to make of his life. Thus a developmental task is that of more clearly defining his dream and finding ways to realize it. It is the mentor who defines the dream and provides needed moral support and encouragement.

The choices of occupation and marriage confront the young man with critical decisions before he has the knowledge and self-understanding to choose wisely. Yet, to delay these decisions, may incur greater costs. Whether one chooses an occupation early or remains undecided, the process of developing an occupation extends throughout the novice phase of early adulthood. No matter how long the couple has known one another prior to marriage, Levinson found they still are not fully prepared for marriage and must strive in later periods to make the marriage work.

The two tasks of the Settling Down period, the fourth period in early adulthood, are to establish one's niche in society, and to work to advance one's personal and social abilities. At the start of the period, the individual is still a junior member in the occupational world, and he depends on others' evaluation of his progress. At the end of this period, from about age 36 to 40, he attempts "to become his own man"; that is, to become a senior member in his occupation and to become less dependent upon other individuals and institutions.

According to Levinson, since no life structure can realize all possibilities—choosing one life course involves rejecting other possibilities—developmental transitions occur during adulthood to permit the emergence of other aspects of the self. From about ages 40 to 45, the Mid-life Transition involves raising difficult questions that reassess one's life. A second task of this period is to begin moving into middle adulthood by testing new choices. And a third task is to deal with polarities that cause division in one's life.

Some of the difficult questions raised during the Mid-life Transition: What have I done with my life? What are my most basic values? What are my talents and am I using or wasting them? What are my goals? The individual recognizes at this time that some of his fundamental beliefs and values are based on illusion and therefore it is necessary to confront them through an intense process, involving grief and disappointment, joy and relief, in relinquishing some of one's illusions.

Some men make major changes during this period, such as divorce, remarriage, change in occupation; others make less dramatic changes but still experience modifications in marital relations, the empty nest (offspring leave home), and changed parental relations: parents are deceased or may now become dependent upon him, if not financially then in everyday matters that they formerly handled by themselves. Erikson speaks of this stage of ego development in the middle years as Generativity vs. Stagnation.

Four polarities are faced in midlife: young/old; creation/destruction; masculine/feminine; attachment/separateness. Although it would appear that one could not have both polar characteristics, these tendencies are not mutually exclusive but can coexist if handled properly. For instance, during this period a man thinks more about his own death and the death of others close to him, considers destructive acts that he committed against others and those committed against him; at the same time he has a desire to become more creative. Thus he can attempt to integrate these polarities during this period. With the young/old polarity, "young" may convey the archetypal symbol of growth, openness, and potential, while "old" may symbolize stability, completion, death. The task is to relinquish some of the youthful qualities and transform other qualities so they can be integrated into one's life.

Similarly, this is a time to seek a better acceptance and integration of the other polarities. A better balance is also sought between the needs of the self and the needs of society; therefore, it is a period of learning to care more about oneself before learning to care more about others. Another problem to be resolved is to modify "the dream" so that one can learn to deal with failure, flawed successes, and illusions by evaluating success and failure in more complex terms based on the quality of experience and the intrinsic value of one's work.

Entering Middle Adulthood is the period from 45 to 50. For some the change is signaled by a "crucial marker event"—a drastic change in job or occupation, marriage or a love affair, a serious illness, or other critical disturbances. Others may show no demonstrable changes. Some men have suffered such irreparable setbacks in childhood or early adulthood that they have few resources to cope with the tasks of this period; others have formed a life structure that is connected better to the world than to the self; and still other men will find this period one of the most fulfilling of the life cycle. Those men better equipped to begin developing an integrated structure for middle adulthood have made sound provisional choices during the Midlife Transition. One must explore what options in life are open to him. Thus an integrated structure may emerge early or late in this period or not at all. Those who develop this structure are less tyrannized by the ambitions, illusions, and passions of their youth. They can also be deeply attached to others and yet still maintain their own identity.

In reassessing *Seasons,* one is struck by the study's implicit normative assumptions that are insufficiently articulated, developed, and defended. The terms "satisfactory" and "satisfactoriness" are frequently used but not developed. The reader, for instance, is informed that the Age Thirty Transition provides an opportunity for creating "a more satisfactory structure," that the final test of the Midlife Transition is the "satisfactoriness" of the structure, and that some men make "satisfactory" provisional choices during the Midlife Transition.[36] Are the choices satisfactory because one is prepared to move on to the next stage? But, as noted earlier, Levinson claimed that no season is more important than any other; yet the thrust of his study would suggest that those who remain in a period beyond a set chronological age manifest arrested growth.

In this case development has a clear direction that is desirable even if the periods do not constitute strict hierarchies. But why should development proceed in this direction? Because these are emergent development characteristics? But this assumes that what is natural and in accord with nature is desirable. By the same token the waste and destruction in nature are also desirable. This line of reasoning also commits one form of the naturalistic fallacy: defining ethical terms in nonethical terms (in this case, nature).

Levinson implies that "integration" is a normative characteristic in some periods of the life cycle; however, despite the ostensible attractiveness of integration as a concept—which, incidentally, is not well developed in

---

[36]*Ibid.,* pp. 84, 194, 278.

the study—the process of integration combines particulars so that they fuse or coalesce and thereby lose their separate identities. In some cases these separate identities should probably be maintained and in other cases integration should be brought about; however, the study does not provide defensible grounds for making such decisions.

Although the study is said to be interdisciplinary, no consideration is given to the biologist's contribution to understanding the aging process. The sample is limited and does not represent those from poor and socially disadvantaged backgrounds. The sample is drawn exclusively from American men and is therefore culture bound. An inadequate account of the methodology is offered, and the study is largely descriptive rather than explanatory. Little information is provided about friendships, parenting, religious beliefs, and political activities of the men in the sample.

Despite these misgivings, the study provides a clearer understanding of American men of these and similar backgrounds, offers a structured and an intelligible approach to development, is innovative in presenting and using new concepts, provides many pertinent insights, and is written with a literary flair.

FOWLER: FAITH AND HUMAN DEVELOPMENT

James Fowler has provided a theory of faith development by describing developmental stages which individuals move through in creating conceptions of ultimate reality and answering such questions as, What is the meaning of life?[37] In developing his theory, Fowler draws upon the works of Piaget, Kohlberg, and Erikson.

"Faith," however, is not given a conventional, but a stipulative, definition in the study—and this makes a great deal of difference for the entire project. Here are some conventional definitions of faith: "firm belief in something for which there is no proof"[38] or "an attitude of belief which goes beyond the available evidence."[39] It is necessary, then, to examine the stipulative definition to ascertain whether Fowler is warranted in

---

[37]James W. Fowler: *Stages of Faith: The Psychology of Human Development and the Quest for Meaning.* San Francisco, Harper & Row, 1981.

[38]*Webster's Ninth New Collegiate Dictionary.* Springfield, Mass., Merrian-Webster, 1983.

[39]Reese, W.L.: *Dictionary of Philosophy and Religion: Eastern and Western Thought.* Atlantic Highlands, N.J., Humanities Press, 1980, p. 166.

employing it in terms of success or failure in generating fruitful and creative ideas.

Faith helps to shield us from our nakedness and provide the courage to face the abyss that surrounds us. It helps us to develop an ultimate environment, a dependable life span. Faith is universal, whether one is a Hindu, Christian, or Marxist. Each person is born with a capacity for faith, but it requires a nurturing environment to grow. Faith is not always religious, as it can apply to nontheists as well. It is the way that individuals find coherence and meaning in their lives; it is a person's way of relating to others against a backdrop of shared meaning and purpose.

What is this quality of life? It is an active mode: a way of trusting, committing, and relating to the world; and by these commitments, as in the family (but not limited to the family), values are conferred that may be of transcendent worth. Thus, linkages are formed with others and institutions which we play a part; these linkages are based on trust and loyalty.

Drawing upon the writings of theologian H. Richard Niebuhr, Fowler identifies three major types of faith-identity relations: polytheistic, henotheistic, and radical monotheistic. A pattern of faith and identity that lacks an organizing center of interest is *polytheistic*. Such persons can never bring all of their concerns to any value commitment or relationship. This type is expressed in the consumer society desire to own anything one wants and have intimate relations with whomever one wishes.

In contrast, the *henotheistic* type invests deeply in a center of value and power, but finds it to be false, inappropriate, and not something of ultimate concern. One invests in projects of self-justification, such as quests for wealth, success, and fame, to bolster the sense of self. In its extreme form, it becomes a fetish in its focus on a narrow and exclusive value center that takes such forms as careerism and workaholism, or where sex and money become gods.

The *radical monotheistic* type finds people relating to one another through bonds of trust and loyalty in which they relinquish their tribal gods and identify with a universal community. It is a regulative point of view that prevents our limited faiths from becoming idolatrous.

Thus faith itself, according to Fowler, is a way of seeing our life in terms of holistic images; our knowledge begins with images and is stored in images. An *image* is a vague inner representation and one's feeling about a state of affairs. Images, therefore, precede concepts and are deeper than them. In answering a question put to us, the first stage of shaping a response is to scan images to discover what we know about something. The world's religions, for instance, evoke the imagery of the ultimate conditions of existence. But because some person's imagery of an "ultimate environment" (the ultimate conditions of existence) may be impersonal, indifferent, or randomly chaotic rather than structured and coherent does not mean that it is not an image of faith. The opposite of faith is nihilism, not doubt. It is the nihilist who despairs in finding any meaning in life and is unable to image a transcendent environment.

Fowler acknowledges his indebtedness to Erikson, Piaget, and Kohlberg; he also indicates that Daniel Levinson's concept of eras enters into his thinking about stages. To acquaint the reader with the first three theorists, he provides a fictional conversation among them about each stage in the life cycle. Erikson's works have formed a backdrop for Fowler's thinking; whereas since Fowler's stage theory is a form of structuralism, he has been influenced more directly by Piaget and Kohlberg. But in contrast to the latter two figures, Fowler has tried to incorporate knowing, valuing, and imaging in each stage. He envisions the stages as generalizable descriptions of integrated sets of knowing and valuing that are invariant. Each stage carries forward and integrates operations of all previous stages. No claim is made that the stages are universal, as they have yet to be tested cross-culturally. The faith stages, however, are neither achievement levels by means of which the worth of persons is evaluated, nor are they therapeutic or educational goals. The educational task is to seek the full values of faith at each stage and help to rework faith when undergoing a transition to the next stage.

From 1972 to 1981 Fowler and his associates conducted 359 taped, in-depth faith development interviews. Each interview lasted two to two and one-half hours and comprised a life review (biography), life-shaping experiences and relationships, present values and commitments, and religious beliefs. Most of the interviews were conducted in Boston and Toronto with persons of differing ages (ranging from 3.5 to 84), sex, race, and religion.

Faith Stages

    Undifferentiated Faith (Infancy)
1. Intuitive-Projective Faith (Early Childhood)
2. Mythic-Literal Faith (School Years)
3. Synthetic-Conventional Faith (Adolescence)

4. Individuative-Reflective Faith (Young Adulthood)
5. Conjunctive Faith (Mid-life and Beyond)
6. Universalizing Faith

Undifferentiated faith is a pre-stage in which the seeds of positive emotions (love, trust) are being formed and contend with various fears about the infant's environment (abandonment, deprivation, and the like). The transition to the first stage emerges with the acquisition of language.

Stage 1 is a fantasy-filled imitative phase in which the child can be permanently influenced by the faith propagated. Thought patterns are fluid and imagination is uninhibited by rational thought. Knowing is dominated by perception, and the imagination creates both positive and negative feelings that thought in later years will have to sort out. The first awareness of sex and death arises at this stage.

Beginning in Stage 2, the child begins to acquire the beliefs, stories, and observances symbolic of one's community. Beliefs and moral rules are interpreted literally. The emergence of concrete operations limits and organizes the previous stage's dominance by imagination. The child learns how to take the perspective of others and to reciprocate. The child can be deeply affected by dramatic tales that tend to be anthropomorphized. Stories and myths are ways of giving coherence to experience, but the stories are not subject to reflection at this stage.

A person's experience extends outside the family in Stage 3. Because of involvement with school or work, peers, the media, and perhaps religion, faith's role is to synthesize values and information from divergent sources to form a sense of identity and a perspective on life. Although this stage arises in adolescence, it becomes a permanent stopping point for many adults. Persons are sensitively attuned to the expectation and judgment of others and are unable to develop autonomous judgment or an independent perspective; the expectations of others become strongly internalized, making it difficult to move to the next stage. The actual transition to the next stage may be precipitated by contradictions between valued sources of authority or experiences that lead to serious reflection about one's beliefs and values.

Although Stage 4 may emerge in young adulthood, for some adults it does not arise until the mid-thirties or forties, and, as noted above, some adults never leave Stage 3. The self in Stage 4 is no longer composed of the viewpoints of other persons and one's roles, but one's self-identity is

differentiated from others. The person translates symbols into conceptual meanings and seeks to banish myths; it is a stage for critical reflection about one's identity and ideology. A transition to the next stage may
occur when the individual, having been inattentive to the unconscious
level, experiences anarchic and disturbing inner voices that conjure
childish past images. A recognition that life is more complex than the
logic that this stage envisions presses one to a more dialectical and
multileveled approach to life.

The self-certainty of Stage 4 gives way to the integration of unrecognized
and suppressed elements that shape Stage 5. Here the individual becomes
open to the deeper self and begins to reclaim and reshape one's past. The
dialectical feature is alive to paradox and seeks to unify opposition. One
can perceive one's own or one's group's most significant meanings while
recognizing their relativity and distortion. Danger, however, lies in one's
life degenerating into complacency or cynical withdrawal in the face of
paradoxical truth. Only a few are able to make the radical actualization
called for in the next stage.

Stage 6 overcomes the paradox by a moral and ascetic actualization.
No longer heeding the dangers to oneself or to one's primary groups, the
individual acts on imperatives of absolute love and justice. These few
individuals at Stage 6 may undergo nonviolent suffering to show respect
for all human beings. They hold open fellowship with persons at any
other stages and faiths. They seek to transform the world in accordance
with a divine and transcendent image. These persons are not perfect, nor
are they identical to Maslow's "self-actualized person" or Rogers' "fully
functioning human being." Representatives of Stage 6 are Gandhi, Martin Luther King, Jr. (in the last years of his life), and Mother Teresa of
Calcutta. Also included are Dag Hammarskjold, Dietrich Bonhoeffer,
Abraham Heschel, and Thomas Merton (this stage is similar to Kohlberg's
Stage Seven).

In augmenting our understanding of this stage theory, Fowler envisions the stages as dynamically connected in a spiral, with each successive stage linked to and adding to the previous ones. Certain life issues
that confront faith recur at each stage; yet each stage approaches these
issues at a new level of complexity. Transitions from one stage are
frequently painful, protracted, and unsuccessful. Although there are
minimum chronological ages below which a stage is not likely to begin,
the transitions are not inevitable or automatic. The *contents* of the
individual's faith (as opposed to its structure) consist of centers of value

(those concerns of greatest worth), images of power (that which sustains the individual in difficult times), and master stories (our interpretive stories about events that affect our lives). By applying this formulation, Fowler is able to explain *conversion* as a change in the contents of faith. It involves recentering our centers of value and images of power and consciously adopting a new set of master stories for reshaping our lives.

A serious problem in some communities is that educational, religious, and governance practices promote a lower stage for adults. In these communities the modal level is in terms of Synthetic-Conventional Faith (Stage 3) or just beyond it. One way Fowler suggests for moving beyond this level is not to shrink from conflict, doubt and struggle. A faith community needs to call forth the strength of each stage of faith.

In assessing Fowler's theory of faith, some problems should be noted. His sample is not random; it is overrepresented by some groups (Jews) and underrepresented by others (Blacks). He admits that no research has been conducted with Eastern religions and traditions. It should be evident, however, that in places he leans heavily on the Judaeo-Christian heritage: in Stage 6 love (New Testament) and justice (Old Testament) are the overriding values. Since Stage 5 and 6 are undergirded by substantive moral and religious views while the stages themselves are considered invariant, one might seriously question the universality of the stage theory (though he does not claim universality). Yet the hierarchical nature implies that later stages are superior to earlier ones. Just as with Kohlberg's theory, one needs an explanation as to how someone can grasp a higher stage in order to make the transition from a lower stage. If one could conceptually grasp the next stage, then the individual would be partly at the higher stage. Perhaps Fowler's ideas about what causes transitions will be of help here.

Some theologians may challenge his distinction between faith, religion, and belief; and his stipulative definition of faith, if rejected, would undermine his study. Others may question whether the dynamics of faith can actually be linked to human development.

Despite these misgivings, Fowler has created the most powerful developmental theory of faith in the literature by organizing his own investigations in light of what he has learned from Erikson, Piaget, and Kohlberg. He has sought to overcome the limitations of the latter two figures' structuralism by creating a place for content and providing in each stage cognitive, affective, and image dimensions. And he has shown how faith can be nurtured and can continue to grow over a lifetime.

LOEVINGER: MILESTONES OF EGO DEVELOPMENT

Mirroring the blind spots of history in general, the focal point for the history of moral development theory has been the study of men. Freud viewed women through stained glass, referring to them as "a dark continent for psychology."[40] Piaget tested his cognitive development theory by utilizing the game of marbles and story-telling techniques with young boys. Kohlberg omitted women from the original sample which became the basis for his longitudinal survey of developmental modes of moral reasoning.[41]

In recent years, certain investigators, primarily female scholars, have attempted to recast moral development by unearthing hidden dimensions of feminine experience. These emergent paradigms are perhaps best represented in Jane Loevinger's model of ego development and in Carol Gilligan's work in psychological theory and women's development. Loevinger and Gilligan seek to reframe Kohlbergean theory; however, their respective positions assume different purposes and therefore create different visions for future constructions of moral development. Whereas Loevinger implies that the broad contours of her theory might apply to males as well as females, Gilligan intimates that her study attempts to redefine moral experience via uniquely feminine perspectives.

Loevinger's inquiry is undergirded by a wide range of prior influences, including the following: psychoanalytic theory; Harry Stack Sullivan's revisions of ego psychology, particularly his notions on interpersonal analysis; theories of character development by Peck and Havighurst; Maslow's formulation of the "self-actualized" person; stage theories of cognitive moral development (Piaget and Kohlberg); and Adler's concept of "style of life," i.e., one's "method of facing problems, opinion about oneself and the problems of life, and the whole attitude toward life."[42]

---

[40]Freud, Sigmund: The question of lay analysis. In *The Standard Edition of the Complete Psychological Works of Sigmund Freud*, (Vol. 20), p. 212.

[41]Kohlberg, Lawrence: The development of modes of moral thinking and choice in the years ten to sixteen. Unpublished doctoral dissertation. University of Chicago, 1958.

[42]Loevinger, Jane and Wessler, Ruth: *Measuring Ego Development*, (Vol. I). San Francisco, Jossey-Bass, 1970, p. 7. Also see Sullivan, Harry Stack: *The Interpersonal Theory of Psychiatry.* New York, Norton, 1953; Peck, Robert F. and Havighurst, Robert J.: *The Psychology of Character Development.* New York, Wiley, 1960; Maslow, Abraham H.: *Motivation and Personality.* New York, Harper, 1954; Piaget, Jean: *The Moral Judgment of the Child.* London, Kegan Paul, 1932; Kohlberg, Lawrence: Development of moral character and moral ideology. In M. Hoffman and L.W. Hoffman (Eds.), *Review of Child Development Research*, (Vol. I). New York, Sage Foundation, 1964, pp. 383–431; and Adler, Alfred: *The Individual Psychology of Alfred Adler*, H.L. Ansbacher and R.R. Ansbacher (Eds.). New York, Basic Books, 1956, p. 174.

Given these complementary foundational sources, Loevinger poses the "search for coherent meanings in experience" to focus her own theoretical inquiry. H.S. Sullivan's theory of ego stability, or *anxiety-gating*, is at the base of Loevinger's general speculations. Sullivan uses the term "anxiety-gating" to show how a person, by *selective inattention*, normally focuses upon patterns of experience which coincide with his/her existing self-system, or ego. Thus the aim of ego maintenance and growth becomes the selective gating out of experiential observations at odds with present ego functions.[43]

These theoretical constructs are made more concrete in Loevinger's studies of women by way of the assessment of "sentence completion" testing. In this evaluation, subjects are given "word stems" (e.g., "I feel sorry . . ." or "When they avoided me . . .") and are then asked to complete each stem in their own words and thoughts (e.g., one might respond to the preceding stems, " . . . for my mistakes" or " . . . I felt hurt and alone"). Notice should be taken that Loevinger's method is a form of psychoanalytic *projective* testing, a relatively unstructured technique which aims at revealing subjects' *affective* as well as cognitive thought patterns. While Kohlberg's methodology is focused at the cognitive level, and mainly attuned to variables in judgmental *reasoning*, Loevinger seeks to tap wider, more subtle, sources of referential response in the person's variegated attitudes and experience. Thus, as with Gilligan's studies, Loevinger's content and process material highlights *emotional dilemmas and conflicts* about morality in ways which escape attention in Kohlberg's discussion.

Loevinger applies the qualitative findings of projective testing to the quantitative measures of psychometrics. On the basis of these findings, she has formulated an eight-stage theory of ego development, sometimes referred to as "milestones of development," as follows (Kohlberg's analogous stages are listed in parentheses):

1. Presocial
2. Symbiotic
3. Impulsive (orientation to Punishment and Obedience)
4. Self-protective (Naively Hedonistic orientation)
5. Conformist ("Good Boy" orientation)
6. Conscientious (orientation to Authority, Law and Order)

---

[43]Loevinger, Jane and Wessler, Ruth: *Measuring Ego Development*, (Vol. I), pp. 7–8.

7. Autonomous (Contractual orientation)
8. Integrated (Principled orientation)[44]

Loevinger places each stage in the context of distinctive dilemmas or conflicts which individuals appear to undergo in an effort to ensure "impulse control" in their "character" development. These parameters bespeak Loevinger's own reliance on "ego strength" and other constructs in ego psychology; moreover, they indicate that she may be mixing "character" development with "moral" development.

Stages 1 and 2 are characterized by the crude emergence of the ego, or self, in a rather undifferentiated state. Here the infant and young child must learn to adapt, to link their *presocial* selves to immediate, but wider, social relationships. Such bonds are first joined in *symbiotic* relations with parent figures. As a result of these ties, the child will normally become "impulsive," e.g., negativistic and self-assertive. At the *impulse* stage (Stage 3), individual thought and action is usually governed by anticipation of reward or punishment. For example, in the child's mind, "good guys give to me, mean ones don't." Loevinger's studies present some case material from adult sentence completion responses which illustrates how individuals carry the baggage of impulsivity into later life:

A woman should always — *keep clean.*
Usually she felt that sex — *is good to me because I get hot.*

Stage 4, or the *self-protective* stage, is arrived at when the person begins to transcend narrow impulsive behavior, thereby incorporating concepts of "right" and "wrong," or blameworthiness, into her character structure. However, feelings of self-control and self-mastery over situations, circumstances, and other persons are still not adequately resolved at this stage. Indeed, there may well be so-called "malignant" signs at this stage, e.g., opportunism, deception, coercion, and manipulation and exploitation of others. Such behavioral signposts correspond to H.S. Sullivan's notion of "malevolent transformation." As examples of "self-protective" ideation, Loevinger cites the following sentence completion responses:

A woman should always — *be alert and on guard.*
A woman's body — *is made for the enjoyment of men.*
My mother and I — *get along when she has money.*

---

[44]*Ibid.*, pp. 10–11. Subsequent sentence-completion illustrations are excerpted from this work. For a succinct view of Loevinger's model in relation to other theories, see Breger, Louis: *From Instinct to Identity: The Development of Personality.* Englewood Cliffs, Prentice-Hall, 1974, pp. 283–294. Breger's analysis is especially instructive in comparing Loevinger with Kohlberg.

The *conformist* stage (Stage 5) reflects Loevinger's findings, roughly in tandem with Kohlberg's broad "conventional-stage" morality, that most people tend to mirror the attitudes, beliefs, and values of those around them. Thus external measures, rather than inner conflictual response, remain at the forefront in this stage. The following sentence completion responses are indicative of the "conformist" period in one's life (which Kohlberg and Loevinger insist most of us never outgrow):

> When I am with a man—*I try to act like a lady.*
> Being with other people—*is the best thing to do.*

Not until Stage 6, the level of *conscientiousness,* does the individual markedly move in the direction of self-decision and personal goal attainment. Loevinger traces this stage to late-adolescent or young-adult kinds of moral thinking and action and claims that it is especially noticeable in college students. It is also a decidedly confusing, tormenting period inasmuch as the young person must weigh past, safer, routes of conventional wisdom with new inroads made by increasing psychological and experiential awareness. That tension is reflected in these sentence completion responses:

> A good mother—*is hard to define.*
> A wife should—*try to understand and sympathize.*
> My conscience bothers me if—*I don't do what I believe is fair or right.*

At the *autonomous* stage (Stage 7), the maturing individual undergoes deepened inner conflict; more sophisticated sensitivity to concrete situations, processes, and change; increasing respect for others' rights and interpersonal relations; and a quickening search for reflective self-fulfillment. Such strivings are articulated in these sentence completion responses:

> My mother and I—*are independent though devoted.*
> When people are helpless—*it is best to aid them to help themselves than to prolong their helplessness and dependency on others.*
> I am—*striving to experience as many things as I can and get a broad view of how the human race lives.*

Finally, an exceedingly small number of people (Loevinger estimates not more than one percent of any given group) enter Stage 8, in which *integrated* reconciliation of previous conflicts and polarizations takes place. These persons are able to deal with paradox and ambiguity, to value justice and idealism, to oppose all manner of prejudice, to manage inner conflict, to appreciate mutuality in relationships, and to do all this with a modicum of existential humor and wisdom. In the unlikely event one should happen to meet such individuals, these vivid examples from Loevinger's sentence completion responses might be helpful for the purpose of identification:

> The worst thing about being a woman—*cannot be generalized, as one woman makes an asset of the same situation decried by another.*
>
> A good mother—*lets go, loves without demanding conformity to her own ideals and standards—and helps to guide if possible.*

Though Loevinger acknowledges that there are doubtless "well-adjusted" people at all her stages and that her scale should not be taken as a "moral IQ" index, she also admits that we live in a "conformist's world" where some feel happy and others fall into various forms of mental illness. Accordingly, Loevinger suggests that *coping mechanisms,* rather than problem solving, may offer the most fruitful tools for moral and psychological well-being in the long run.

Even though her theory makes use of a rich variety of sources (a circumstance which might be at the root of some of her methodological problems), Loevinger grants that there are numerous difficulties in her investigation. First, there may in fact be no necessary correspondence between "a given bit of behavior" as exemplified in the sentence-completion exercises and those attitudes which might underlie any such given responses. That is, Loevinger casts her theory at a "probabilistic" level. Second, there are doubtless myriad kinds of development proceeding along with ego development, thus making for fuzzy boundaries of distinction among such areas as "cognitive," "psychosexual," and "moral" development. (Indeed, the term "ego" itself represents a very tenuous borderland for conceptual analysis.) Next, there are companion difficulties in ascertaining distinct levels of development since most behavior is typically manifested at more than one level. Moreover, Loevinger recognizes the related problem of assigning behavioral and attitudinal signs to any particular developmental level. Finally, she is admirably honest in acknowledging perhaps the weakest link in her entire theory:

> No behavioral task can be guaranteed to display just what one wants to know about ego level. Neither a structured test nor an unstructured test carries a guarantee.... There is always a chance that a person can conceal all ...[45]

---

[45]Loevinger, Jane and Wessler, Ruth: *Measuring Ego Development,* (Vol. I), p. 9.

Indeed, we all may sometimes hide our underlying motives and the reasons for our ordinary behavior in the everyday life of moral action.

GILLIGAN: IN A DIFFERENT VOICE

Carol Gilligan has challenged Kohlberg's theories in light of her own research on women. While Gilligan's model of women's moral development is not in finished form, still needs to be further tested, and is couched in highly speculative, intuitive language, it nonetheless counterposes a rich tapestry of *particular social and personal context* alongside Kohlberg's more abstractly contemplative universe of discourse. The basic thrust of Gilligan's thesis underscores a language of care, responsibility, and not wanting to hurt others in women's presumably unique moral thema and moral vision.

According to Gilligan, women speak "in a different voice" than men. Extrapolating on Kohlberg's studies, Gilligan hypothesizes that women's language is substantially one of caring and interpersonal responsibility whereas men's dialect seems to be framed in terms of individual rights, liberties, duties, and their attendant protection. Some critics have argued that the rather warm reception of Kohlberg's paradigm may be explained in part by its tendency to "reinforce current dominant views about pluralistic democracy and justice as fairness."[46] In other words, Kohlberg's model of justice may be part and parcel of that strong core of "liberal individualism" so popular in Western culture.[47]

How does Gilligan conceptualize the development of "self" and "other"? She takes an evolutionary stance attuned to the subjective passages of those women whom she interviews in her studies. (To her credit, Gilligan's action research is carried on with women who *actually* face extraordinary personal moral dilemmas, e.g., whether to have an abortion. Her technique seems more realistic than the imaginary, hypothetical questions posed in Kohlberg's experiments.) The fluid growth sequence in women's ethic of care appears to follow: (1) "an initial focus on caring for the self in order to ensure survival"; (2) "a transitional phase in which this judgment is criticized as selfish"; and (3) "a new understanding of the

---

[46]Sichel, Betty A.: Moral development and education: men's language of rights and women's language of responsibility. *Contemporary Education Review*, 2:34, Spring, 1983.

[47]See Pateman, Carole: The "disorder of women": women love, and the sense of justice. *Ethics*, 91:20–34, 1980, for a similar assessment of Rousseau, Freud, and other major figures in Western thought.

connection between self and others which is articulated by the concept of responsibility."[48]

Gilligan further contends that this "new understanding" of relatedness would be vitiated if one were to gauge women's moral development solely with reference to Kohlberg's theoretical interpretations. In her interviews with 11-year-old children, Amy and Jake, Gilligan attempts to show how Amy's evident moral virtues would be minimized if she were judged by Kohlberg's categories. Using Kohlberg's classic Heinz case (stealing from the druggist to save the life of one's spouse), Gilligan's interviews reveal different responses from Amy and Jake. The latter solves the Heinz issue in a manner akin to the algebraic gymnastic he performs in mathematics class: who has the property right and what is fair for the individual? Amy, on the other hand, is more intent on making sure that Heinz and his wife do not suffer in their relationship as a result of any theft. On Kohlberg's scale of values, Amy's compassionate logic would be insufficiently informed by principles of moral *reasoning*, which presumably emphasize fairness, justice, and rights.

Gilligan and associates' more recent work challenges the developmental model that equates adulthood with a justice perspective, and maturity with separation, self-sufficiency, and independence. She discerns a need to reconsider adolescent development because girls have been neglected, extant studies are often overlooked or not cited, and Piagetian theories of cognitive development provide an inadequate rationale for this population. Care concerns are a focus of a coherent moral perspective rather than a deficiency in women's moral reasoning or a subordinate set of moral concerns within a justice framework. She found that North American adolescents and adults who participated in her and her colleagues' studies raised considerations of both care and justice in describing moral conflicts; yet they focused primarily on either one or the other. The two approaches, however, are not opposites or mirror images of one another (with justice uncaring and care unjust), but involve different ways of organizing problems and different reasoning strategies.[49] The pattern was not gender-specific but gender-related, suggesting two moral voices as different ways of viewing the world. Within the care perspective, being dependent does not mean helplessness,

---

[48]Gilligan, Carol: *In a Different Voice: Psychological Theory and Women's Development.* Cambridge: Harvard U.P., 1982, p. 74.

[49]Gilligan, Carol; Ward, J.V.; Taylor, J.M.; Bardige, B. (Eds.): *Mapping the Moral Domain.* Cambridge, MA: Harvard University Press, 1988, Prologue.

powerlessness, and lack of control; instead it signifies that one can have an effect on others, as well as recognizing that interdependence empowers the self and others. The activities of care—being there, listening, helping, understanding—assume a moral dimension in which one does not turn away from need.[50]

Gilligan summarizes three studies with comparable designs that sampled male and female subjects matched for high economic status. All participants were questioned about decision situations involving moral conflict in which they were asked to describe the situation, uncover the conflicts, report and assess their decisions. The findings indicated that 69 percent of the respondents (55 out of 80) used both orientations (Care and Justice). Nevertheless, the Care Focus is much more likely to occur in the moral dilemma of a woman, while the Justice Focus is more likely in the dilemma of a man.[51]

Gilligan and others also studied adolescent girls at the Emma Willard School in Troy, New York. She found that teenage girls and adult women faced a dilemma whether to respond to others and abandon themselves or respond to themselves and abandon others. Adolescence, as other studies have shown, is likely to be a critical period for girls when they tend to first manifest such psychological difficulties as increasing episodes of depression, speaking more disparagingly than boys in appraising themselves, and exhibiting more disturbances in self-image. These syndromes seem to emerge from problems of connection rather than problems of separation.[52]

A study of thirty-four Emma Willard girls was made of the convergence of unfairness and not-listening contexts. For unfairness, girls were asked to tell about a situation in which someone was treated unfairly, and were questioned as to what made it unfair and what was the fair thing to do. For not listening, they were questioned as to how they determined someone was not being listened to, and what would have made it possible for that person to be heard.

A difference was observed in the responses of ninth/tenth and twelfth-grade girls. A typical ninth or tenth grader located unfairness in public

---

[50]Gilligan, Carol: Remapping the moral domain: New images of self in relationship. In ibid, ch. 1.

[51]Gilligan, Carol and Attanucci, Jane: Two moral orientations. In ibid, ch. 4.

[52]Gilligan, Carol; Lyons, Nona; Hanmer, Trudy J. (Eds.): *Making Connections.* Cambridge, MA: Harvard University Press, 1990, Preface.

contexts and not listening largely in private contexts of family and friendship. Conversely, twelfth graders described not listening in relation to public authority figures and unfairness in relation to peers. Questions about unfairness usually elicited moral indignation, while questions about not listening tended to elicit observations of psychological need. At higher grade levels girls showed a convergence in the content and tone of unfairness and not listening responses by intermingling moral passion with a concern for responsive relationships. The two concepts tended to be defined in terms of one another: fairness as responsiveness to needs and listening as showing respect.[53] Overall, Gilligan claims that her studies of women's moral development reveal a progression from an egocentric to a normative or conventional to an autonomous or reflective position.[54]

Gilligan has offered evidence of two modes of moral development and perceiving the world, and she has drawn attention to the neglect of both women's thinking and research studies of adolescent girls. She has also directly challenged such dominant paradigms as those advanced by Piaget and Kohlberg.

Gilligan, in her early work, admits that her samples are "small and nonrepresentative".[55] In her study at Emma Willard School, conclusions from few cases are generalized to the majority of girls at the school and, by extension, to most adolescent girls. No mention is made of the school's recruitment and socialization practices to provide a broader context for the study and to make findings more meaningful.[56] Some critics have charged that her earlier study, *In A Different Voice,* is biased and methodologically inadequate.[57] Her series of studies, *Mapping the Moral Domain,* have been found to be "exceedingly repetitious", with each chapter recapitulating her earlier research. One needs to ask: Why is it important culturally to assign different moralities to men and women? What social relations are legitimated by such gender constructions of

[53]Bernstein, Elizabeth and Gilligan, Carol: Unfairness and not listening: Converging themes in Emma Willard Girls' Development. In ibid, pp. 147–161.

[54]Gilligan, Carol; Rogers, Annie; Brown, Lyn Mirel: Epilogue: Soundings and development. In ibid, pp. 314–334.

[55]Murphy, J.M. and Gilligan, Carol: Moral development in late adolescence and adulthood: A critique and reconstruction of Kohlberg's theory. *Human Development,* 23: 84, 1980.

[56]Review of *Making Connections,* by Mary Percival Maxwell. *Queens Quarterly* 97, 698–99, Winter 1990.

[57]Colby, A. and Damon, W.: Listening to a different voice: A review of Gilligan's *In A Different Voice.* Merrill-Palmer Quarterly, 29, 473–81, 1983.

reality, and whose needs do they serve?[58] Linking moral modes only to gender serves to essentialize gender, "removing it from the context of relationships, discourse, culture, societal structure, and processes of historical formulation."[59]

KARDINER AND BERRY: CROSS-CULTURAL HUMAN DEVELOPMENT

Cross-cultural human development envisions behavior as a product of cultures and seeks to assess how sociocultural variables influence human behavior. In that quest researchers sometimes focus on behavioral differences across cultures and at other times search for universal patterns of behavior. Researchers seek to account for the apparent differences in personality characteristics from one society to another. Ultimately the goal is to discover the relation between culture and behavior.

Ralph Linton, an anthropologist, and Abram Kardiner, a psychoanalyst, developed in seminars at Columbia University a number of important ideas for culture-and-personality studies. Kardiner suggested that in every culture a *basic personality structure* is produced by certain shared cultural experiences.[60] Though it is a derivative of the psychological concept of personality, it is based upon a study of culture rather than the individual. It represents a constellation of personality traits consonant with the institutions comprising the culture. Personalities are shaped by common cultural experiences. These shared experiences derive from primary institutions, which have to do with making a living, the composition of the family, and the customs of childrearing. The basic personality structure generates secondary institutions that are created to satisfy and reconcile the needs and conflicts of the basic personality structure. Secondary institutions, which include ritual, religion, and folklore, are considered secondary because they evidently stem from the basic personality structure.

Kardiner rejects the concepts of human nature and Oedipus complex because they assume universality. He assumes that the biological needs

[58]Mednick, M.: On the politics of psychological constructs: Stop the bandwagon I want to get off. *American Psychologist,* 44, 1118–1123, 1989.

[59]Broughton, J.M.: Women's rationality and men's virtues: A critique of gender dualism in Gilligan's theory of moral development. *Social Research* 50, 635, 1983.

[60]Kardiner, Abram: *The Individual and His Society: The Psychodynamics of Primitive Social Organization.* New York: Columbia University Press, 1939.

in the different cultures are quite similar but the external realities differ. These external realities consist of the natural environment and the institutional system. Adjustment to differing external realities create divergent forms of adaptation and thought processes. In Zuni culture mutual dependency is the expectation of every individual; in Kwakiutl, mutual dependency is limited solely to subsistence needs; in Chuckchee, it is unavailable. Where one culture comes into contact with another, only those traits are diffused that are helpful to or not incompatible with the basic personality structure. One may thereby make general predictions as to the likely reactions of a culture to a given innovation.

Not all psychological anthropologists utilize Kardiner's scheme, but most assume a set of typical personality characteristics, whether called "basic personality," "national character," or "modal personality." Also most accept Kardiner's assumption that the typical personality is produced by certain aspects of cultural experience, especially the forms of childrearing.

The concept of basic personality structure portrays only typical personalities and not deviant behavior; consequently, the concept of *modal personality* was developed to portray not only the typical personality but also the range of variation. It represents a statistical statement offering a frequency distribution of different personality characteristics in a culture. But this requires measurement of actual personality characteristics rather than observations about the culture.

Basic personality structure is an abstraction and a derivation of culture. The secondary effects attributed to its action on the individual and culture are likely to be questioned. Knowledge of the actual personality characteristics of individuals of a culture are therefore to be gained through an independent series of studies.

Basic personality structure suggests that those who conform to the desired personality traits will be considered moral in a given culture, depending upon the degree of compliance. Those with exemplary compliance will likely be made models for the young to emulate. Those deviating from the basic personality structure will likely be considered immoral, especially in a relatively homogeneous society, and will be appropriately punished or reformed according to the applicable mores.

A number of salient criticisms, however, have been made of culture-and-personality studies. Wallace found in the research a widespread tendency to conceive societies as culturally homogeneous and to expect individuals to share a uniform nuclear character. He claimed that the "core personalities" produced by this type of research were either abstractions from descriptions of individual personalities or deductions from cultural descriptions. Instead, he holds that much diversity can be found within cultures and this diversity is neither pathogenic nor nonfunctional.[61]

Another problem in this research stems from its heavy dependence on projective techniques. Lindzey reviewed many of these studies that employed the Rorschach test cross-culturally and concluded that the technique imposes the language of pathology; the data are difficult to quantify and treat statistically; overt behaviors are ignored; and the validity of the scoring procedures is dubious.[62]

A different and promising approach in cross-cultural studies developed by John W. Berry is to create a model that attempts to structure the interrelationships among three classes of variables: ecological, adaptive, and behavioral.[63] The model avoids deterministic and linear weaknesses of previous cross-cultural models by treating each of the modeled relationships as probabilistic and by employing feedback relations for most of the elements in the model. Cultural and behavioral variables are considered to be adapting to ecology; adaptive relationships are probabilistic, and are subject to empirical testing.

Berry's premise is that ecological variables are the prime movers of culture and behavior. Ecological variables include climate, water supply, soil conditions, and terrain; these variables combine to influence a society's food production system. Decisions about how a society feeds its members are influenced by natural conditions (e.g., a decision to rely upon meat from animals depends upon availability, climate, water supply, and the like). A society's degree of food accumulation is correlated with other characteristics. High-food-accumulating societies tend to be relatively densely populated and sedentary, while low-food-accumulating societies are composed of less dense, migratory populations.

Adaptive variables are the sociocultural and organismic characteristics of cultures. The sociocultural characteristics include all of the human institutions to enable populations to survive in a given ecology. These would include political and kinship systems as well as socialization

---

[61]Wallace, A.F.C.: Culture and Personality. New York: Random House, 1961.

[62]Lindzey, G.: *Projective Techniques and Cross-Cultural Research.* New York: Appleton-Century-Crofts, 1961.

[63]Berry, J.W.: Ecological and Cultural factors in spatial perceptual development. *Canadian Journal of Behavioral Science, 3:* 324–336, 1971; An ecological approach to cross-cultural psychology. *Nederlands Tijdschrift voor de Psychologic, 30:* 51–84, 1975; *Human Ecology and Cognitive Style.* Beverly Hills, CA: Sage, 1976.

mechanisms. Ecological forces will determine whether a society is sedentary or migratory, and kinship systems will likely differ in the two types of ecological adaptations.

Organismic variables, the second type of adaptive variables, consists of adaptative responses of a population over generations that is genetic or physiological. Genetic differences across subpopulations are organismic adaptations to ecological pressure. These differences may take the form of differential susceptibility to disease. Organismic and sociocultural variables may interact with one another, as in the case that cultural taboos regarding certain foods may have originally had a genetic basis.

Behavioral variables, the third class of variables, may also be called individual-development variables and include all measurable aspects of individual behavior that can be linked to ecological or adaptive variables or both. Testable predictions can be derived on cross-cultural task performances on tests that measure differentiation, which refers to the individual's ability to measure parts from the whole field in which they are embedded.[64] In nomadic hunting and gathering societies where population density and sociocultural stratification are low, and where socialization emphasizes assertion, one may expect high levels of psychological differentiation. Conversely, in sedentary agricultural societies where population density and sociocultural stratification are high, and where socialization emphasizes compliance, low levels of psychological differentiation may be expected. People from low-food-accumulating societies engage in hunting and fishing, activities that require a high degree of spatial skills. Groups that are highly differentiated on special-cognitive tasks are also highly independent; those undifferentiated are more susceptible to social influence.

Because Berry's model indicates the great influence on human behavior of ecological and adaptive variables, the model would imply that morality and moral development arise as adaptive mechanisms in response to a particular set of ecological variables (as is evident in the above differences in nomadic and agricultural societies). Socialization processes in agricultural societies usually emphasize responsibility, obedience, and nurturance; whereas in nomadic cultures achievement, self-reliance, and independence are stressed.

---

[64]Witkin, H.A.: A cognitive style approach to cross-cultural research. *International Journal of Psychology, 2*, 233–250, 1967; Witkin, H.A. and Berry, J.W.: Psychological differentiation in cross-cultural perspective. *Journal of Cross-Cultural Psychology, 6*, 4–87, 1975.

Central to Berry's research is theory building, with the empirical aspects in the service of theoretical components. The theory has served as a guide to the next research steps; in turn, the findings have contributed to an elaboration of the theory and further development of testable hypotheses. To test his hypotheses, Berry extensively studied ten cultures varying in the form of economic adaptation, sedentariness, and contact with industrial societies. The findings provide strong support for the hypotheses and illuminate role differentiation within and across cultures.

Although Berry has sought to avoid a deterministic model, his framework is premised on ecological variables as the prime movers of culture and behavior rather than merely interacting with one another. Moreover, some cultural elements—such as the arts and religion—are not directly linked to ecological variables in that they are derived through cognitive and creative processes.

KURTINES: PSYCHOSOCIAL THEORY

William M. Kurtines and Associates have developed a psychosocial role theory that views human behavior as rule governed and emphasizes freedom and creativity in human behavior and development.[65] The theory is more inclusive than maturational and learning processes by encompassing psychosocial competencies (linguistic, cognitive, communicative, and sociomoral). A central focus is the role of co-constructive communicative processes in the ontogenesis of sociomoral knowledge and understanding. The approach to moral behavior and development is based on a rule-governed perspective to account for person and situation effects on moral choices and decisions.

Kurtines finds that present research on person variables oversimplifies the complex interaction between the person as moral agent and the network of socially defined rules and roles. As such models are limited

---

[65]Kurtines, William M.: Moral behavior as rule-governed behavior: A psychosocial role-theoretical approach to moral behavior and development. In Kurtines, William M. and Gewirtz, Jacob L. (Eds.): *Morality, Moral Behavior, and Moral Development.* New York: Wiley, 1984, pp. 303–324; Kurtines, William M.: Sociomoral behavior and development from a rule-governed perspective: Psychosocial theory as a nomotic science. In Kurtines, William M. and Gewirtz, Jacob L.: *Moral Development Through Social Interaction.* New York: Wiley, 1987, pp. 149–194; and Kurtines, William M.; Maycock, Ellen; Pollard, Steven R.; Lanza, Teresita; Carlo, Gustavo: Social and moral development from the perspective of psychosocial theory. In Kurtines, William M. and Gewirtz, Jacob (Eds.): *Handbook of Moral Behavior and Development.* Hillsdale, NJ: Lawrence Erlbaum, 1991, vol. 1, pp. 303–333.

to personal variables, they do not provide a theoretically meaningful account of situation variables.

Psychosocial theory draws upon open systems theory, traditional role theory, and rule-governed behavior. The theory postulates four assumptions: human behavior is (1) rule governed; (2) purposive or intentional; (3) anthropomorphic (human beings are self-directed and employ rules to achieve goals); and (4) social. Morality is viewed as providing system maintenance and integration. Moral dilemmas arise from conflicts between rules and roles in the system; moral judgments are decisions concerning the relative priority of moral rules; and moral conduct is behavior that is consistent with the rules.

Drawing from systems theory, the notion of a social system is a major operational concept. A social system is an open-ended, socially constructed, structurally integrated, recurrent cycle of social events. The two basic units of social systems are rules and roles. The underlying structure of morality can be defined by: Level I, moral rules that prescribe or prohibit certain acts; Level II, the reciprocal moral rights existing between role occupants in the system; and Level III, the moral principles that underlie the rules and rights. Principles of utility and justice are found at Level III. The approach assumes a structural isomorphism between the basic principles that structure the social component of morality and the basic principles of the individual's thought and reasoning about morality. In addition to the principles of utility and justice, the systems perspective adds the pragmatic principle that defines an act as good if it is more practical, useful, or efficient than alternate acts. At a cognitive level, these three principles serve as cognitive structures or schemata to organize and unify the individual's social knowledge. They do so by providing structure for the individual's moral rule repertoire and for resolving conflict among the rules.

Psychosocial role theory is similar to social psychological theories proposed by Erikson, Fromm, and others; it differs in its focus on human behavior as rule governed. It suggests that human behavior is not regulated by laws governing natural phenomena but complies with rules that are individually and collectively created.

Psychosocial theory is conceived as a nomotic science. Nomotics is the science of human rules and rule systems. Nomotic research consists of two domains: reconstructive and constructive. Reconstructive research focuses on the reconstruction of already existing implicit knowledge and is retrospective in nature; it seeks to identify universal structures of sociomoral knowledge. Reconstructive research has been successfully conducted in theoretical linguistics (by Chomsky), genetic epistemology (Piaget), and communication theory (Habermas). In contrast, constructive research seeks to identify the process by which novel forms of sociomoral knowledge emerge. Constructive research is more prospective and process-oriented rather than retrospective and structure-oriented. Reconstructive research cannot derive hypotheses for new forms of nomotic knowledge, as such hypotheses would assume that future nomotic knowledge will be similar to past forms. Constructive research focuses on the form of new nomotic knowledge rather than the outcome of the process.

As rules are open to human construction, ontogenic change in sociomoral knowledge can no longer be viewed as strictly a product of maturation and learning. Such changes can also be conceptualized as part of a formative evolutionary process as well as a developmental process. A distinction can be made between an understanding of rules and rule systems (competence) and the rise or application of rules (performance). Competent rule users understand a variety of things without being able to provide an account of the rules or criteria on which their performances are based.

The full range of psychosocial competence comprises linguistic, cognitive, and communicative competencies. These competencies, as well as sociomoral ones, are needed in the reproduction of society. Performances involving higher level competencies encompass lower level ones, but performances involving lower level competencies do not involve higher level operations.

Four developmental levels are organized in terms of a psychosocial perspective. Level 1: Presubjective (Infancy 0–2) finds the infant at the preverbal level and at the sensorimotor stage. Communicative action is largely nonnormative goal-oriented acts structured around the sensorimotor level. The sociomoral orientation is premoral.

At Level 2: Egocentric-Subjective (Childhood 2–7), the child has sufficient linguistic competence for verbal interaction and cognitively is at the preoperational stage. The child is gaining role-playing skills and engages in ordinary communicative action and goal-oriented action. Sociomoral competence is heteronomous and uncritical and, though the child gains an understanding of rules, the rules are viewed as externally imposed. The child is egocentric by focusing on subjective needs and interests.

Linguistic competence becomes fully developed at Level 3: Sociocentric-

Intersubjective (Preadolescent 7–12). The preadolescent's cognitive competence is concrete operational, exhibits decentered thinking and role playing skills whose focus is sociocentric. The preadolescent manifests some ability for discursive communicative action in the sense of willingness to suspend judgment on problematic claims. Sociomoral rules are viewed as intersubjectively shared rather than externally imposed and the sociomoral orientation is autonomous. The psychosocial perspective is sociocentric and oriented toward intersubjectively shared needs, interests, and values.

At Level 4: Critical (Adolescent–Adult 12–+) the youth/adult is at the stage of formal operations. The youth/adult has the abilities to be more detached from roles and to take the perspective of a neutral third party. The individual has the capacity to engage in all levels of communicative action. As for sociomoral competence, the individual can participate in critical-hypothetical thinking and critical-discursive communication. Level 4, therefore, defines psychosocial maturity.

Although moral judgment has been generally conceived as a unitary process, a systems perspective requires two different types of judgment: behavioral and system. A behavioral decision is qualitative, regulates behavior, and offers a choice between acting or not acting (as between lying or not lying). Behavioral decisions are teleological in terms of the consequences serving as decision criteria.

A distributive decision, in contrast, involves the allocation of resources and provides the decision maker with a choice of two or more distributions of some activity or thing within the system. Distributive decisions involve the allotment or distribution of rights, obligations, or sanctions, rewards or punishments in terms of amount or quantity. Such decisions are deontological by their emphasis on fairness of the distribution rather than on the consequences.

Several research studies were conducted on moral decision making. The first research study hypothesized that teleological principles would be preferred in behavioral decisions and deontological principles in distributive decisions. The study developed a set of six simulated moral situations in which three involved a behavioral decision about lying, breaking a promise, and stealing, while the other three required a distributive decision about responsibility, reward, or punishment. Each distributive decision involved a conflict between merit and need. Respondents were asked in all six situations which of three principles (justice, utility, pragmatism) justified their decisions. The results showed that the principle of justice was most frequently used and pragmatism least used. The analyzed data support the hypothesis of situation specificity in the use of moral principles.

The second study consisted of testing a Measure of Moral Value Preference (MMVP) with 83 undergraduate volunteers. MMVP assesses individual differences in rule usage employing methods of self-report, recognition, and recall, and includes individual difference scales for Justice, Utility, and Pragmatism. Several analyses indicated that the value preference component has adequate psychometric properties.

MMVP was employed in a third study with 64 undergraduate student volunteers in which the dependent variable was moral choice in the six simulated moral situations. The MMVP was scored for Justice, Utility, and Pragmatism. Respondents were asked to make behavioral decisions using a 100-point scale on the likelihood and severity of the projected consequences. Distributive judgment situations required respondents on a 100-point scale to make judgments as to the relative importance of need and merit. The results of regression analysis showed, among other things, that the total amount of variance explained by both sets of variables was generally high, and that the total variance was higher in the distributive decision situations than the behavioral.[66]

Kurtines and Associates have developed a host of other research measures (designated by the term Sociomoral Competence Scale) for purposes of determining basic dimensions of sociomoral knowledge and understanding and to measure sociomoral competence.[67] They have also applied psychosocial theory to moral education.[68]

Psychosocial theory differs with the view that moral development is the primary goal of moral education; rather, it is considered only one of the goals and is part of a broader framework of education for democracy that includes a full range of competencies: linguistic, cognitive, communicative, and sociomoral. The process of social evolution is not dependent as is biological evolution on random variation but changes as an outcome of problem-solving activity, and such change, through feedback, creates new forms of knowledge. The reproduction of society requires

---

[66]Kurtines; Moral behavior as rule-governed behavior.

[67]Kurtines, et al.: Social and moral development from the perspective of psychosocial theory.

[68]Pollard, Steven R.; Kurtines, William M.; Carlo, Gustavo; Dancs, Mary; Maycock, Ellen: Moral education from the perspective of psychosocial theory. In Kurtines, William M. and Gewirtz, Jacob L. (Eds.): *Handbook of Moral Behavior and Development.* Hillsdale, NJ: Lawrence Erlbaum, 1991, vol. 3, pp. 289–315.

the transmission of knowledge across generations. Since continuity of culture is essential for any society, socialization should be one of the goals of education. But modern education should also go beyond socialization to facilitate the creation of new knowledge and understanding. Education should be both a process of cultural transmission and the development of skills and competencies. These competencies would include highly technical linguistic and cognitive competencies. Thus the development of competence is also a goal of education. Another goal is to facilitate the use or practice of modes of critical thinking and discussion.

Though psychosocial theory draws upon both essentialism and progressivism, it is consistent with Dewey's ideas about education for democracy but seeks to carry his thought further. Education is needed not only for democratic life but because critical thinking and discussion is the embodiment of the democratic ideal. Thus education for democracy aims at the development and use of competence in critical thinking and discussion. Democracy requires the institutionalization of democratic modes of thought and discussion. Education for citizenship should use current sociomoral-political issues as the content for learning modes of critical thinking and discussion. To this end, training exercises titled Developing and Applying Critical Skills Exercise were developed for resolving conflict through communication. Value conflict was used as content for organizing lessons and teaching critical thinking and discussion skills. The study found that subjects in the experimental training condition engaged in more discussion than the control condition.

One may infer that psychosocial theory and its educational thought is a relativist position. Kurtines and Gewirtz briefly surveyed objectivistic or absolutist moral and epistemological orientations versus relativistic orientations since the ancient Greeks and concluded that while an objectivist orientation has characterized Western thought through much of its history, the rise of modern science and other intellectual developments have led to a relativistic orientation.[69] The current diversity of views in moral development theory, ranging from objectivism to radical relativism, is symptomatic of the moral uncertainty of our age and this pluralism the authors predict will prevail until a synthesis occurs, if such a synthesis is possible, of relativistic and probabilistic epistemology. But the authors do not explore contemporary problems in relativism and

---

[69]Kurtines, William M. and Gewirtz, Jacob L.: Certainty and morality: Objectivistic versus relativistic approaches. In Kurtines and Gewirtz, *Morality, Moral Behavior, and Moral Development,* pp. 3–23.

thereby overlook the entangled, problematic status of this epistemological and moral position.[70] Kurtines further confuses the issue elsewhere when he draws upon Kierkegaard and Sartre to support his view that the individual, not systems or principles, must bear the responsibility for moral decisions and action.[71] Their position, however, is a form of subjectivism rather than relativism; moreover, Sartre asserts that " . . . my freedom is the unique foundation of values and that *nothing*, absolutely nothing, justifies me in adopting this or that particular value, this or that particular scale of values."[72]

A number of other problems can be found in psychosocial theory. The theory largely neglects the affective domain. Nor is it clear that the developmental stages and their characteristics have been confirmed by research other than the cognitive aspects drawn from Piaget.

The educational ideas show neither the originality nor the rigor of the developmental theory, as they provide a reconciliation of essentialist and progressive ideas by combining content and critical thinking and then slightly reformulating Dewey's thinking on democracy and education. This line of thought needs to be updated with more recent formulations.[73]

Nevertheless, psychosocial theory is a significant explanatory system that is more inclusive than cognitive moral development theory by providing linguistic, communicative, and sociomoral competencies as well as cognitive ones. It shows originality, is highly systematic and rigorous, demonstrates strong explanatory value, does not oversimplify complex behavior, provides heuristically valuable research instruments, and achieves some integration of the latest thinking from multiple disciplines.

---

[70]See: Krausz, Michael and Meiland, Jack W. (Eds.): *Relativism: Cognitive and Moral.* Notre Dame, IN: Notre Dame University Press, 1982; Harris, James F.: *Against Relativism.* LaSalle, IL: Open Court, 1992.

[71]Kurtines, William M.: Moral behavior as rule-governed behavior, pp. 320–322.

[72]Sartre, Jean-Paul: *Being and Nothingness.* New York: Washington Square Press, 1975, p. 76.

[73]See: Peters, R.S.: *Ethics and Education.* London: Routledge & Kegan Paul, 1966; Barber, Benjamin R.: *An Aristocracy of Everyone:* New York: Ballantine Books, 1992; and Gutmann, Amy: *Democratic Education.* Princeton, NJ: Princeton University Press, 1987.

Chapter 6

ISSUES IN MORAL DEVELOPMENT THEORY

A SALIENT characteristic of moral development theory is its heterogeneity and diversity of systems and perspectives. Each system seeks
to provide compelling reasons for its adoption by overcoming alleged
weaknesses of prevailing systems by means of its inclusiveness, explanatory power, predictive ability, testability, fruitfulness, consistency, and
simplicity. But would it not be advantageous for the field to seek more
inclusive and integrative theories by combining existing ones and dis-
couraging the proliferation of new ones? Alfred Baldwin believes that all
the topics he surveyed in six child development theories are important,
the theories do not conflict, and it is therefore possible to develop an
integrated theory. To do so, one has to develop a neutral language in
which the concepts can be described without distortion. Such a language
should be unambiguous and be able to express any content, whether true
or not. He believes that stimulus-response language is a relatively neutral one, but that it is more important to be able to describe accurately
rather than be restricted to operationalizable concepts. But he bypasses
the problem of whether behavioral events are to be described in molecu-
lar or molar terms. Both thoughts and feelings should be accepted, with
mental events and inhibitory events construed as hypothetical constructs.
Some consensus among theories is found in the conviction of a primitive,
noncognitive functioning that is superseded by an advanced cognitively
mediated process. Baldwin, after considering other developmental
concepts, concludes that his proposal is only an incomplete sketch.[1]

Others are less sanguine about integrating theories. Some theories are
bold and speculative, while others are limited and precise; they address
different levels of phenomena, from simple reflexes to complex moral
reasoning. "Any attempt to integrate all the theories would be foolish at
best, and misleading at worst," says Patricia Miller.[2] We would agree

---

[1]Baldwin, Alfred L.: *Theories of Child Development* (2nd ed.). New York, Wiley, 1980, ch. 21.

[2]Miller, Patricia H.: *Theories of Developmental Psychology.* San Francisco, W.H. Freeman, 1983, p. 382.

that, even if desirable, such an integration does not appear to be presently feasible; yet these caveats should not discourage those with special insight from undertaking this difficult task.

But why are there many rather than few theories of moral development? One explanation is that of cross-fertilization. Until the early 1940s developmental psychology was primarily descriptive and normative. But with the events leading up to World War II, many Jewish intellectuals fled Europe and began careers in the United States. The dissemination of these European ideas led to a greater emphasis upon explanation and promoted plurality of perspectives.[3] But the abundance of theories can also be explained by the complexity of the world and human nature, the variety of plausible explanations for phenomena, competition among theoreticians, changes in outlook during different historical periods, and the discovery of problems that cannot adequately be explained by existing theories. An additional reason could possibly be a will to power. As Nietzsche observed, life is largely a will to power, the feeling that one is in command of oneself and of the future. In this quest one finds the values which most people accept are inadequate and one must adopt a new and, in many cases, an opposite set of values.[4] But this Nietzscheian hypothesis would need to be confirmed through studies of numerous psychohistories that presently are unavailable.

THEORY DEVELOPMENT

What is theory? Numerous definitions are available and generally tend to reflect the author's philosophy, although some of the definitions have a family resemblance. The social and behavioral sciences were greatly influenced by the Vienna Circle of the 1920s and the program propounded by the logical positivists. Though positivism began in the nineteenth century with Comte and Mill, it was developed more thoroughly and disseminated more widely by the Vienna Circle. The movement's first phase was taken up with formulating a verification principle and dealing with initial problems of logic and epistemology. During the second phase in the 1940s, corrections were made to over-

---

[3]Dixon, Roger A. and Lerner, Richard M.: A history of systems in developmental psychology. In Bornstein, Marc H. and Lamb, Michael E.: *Developmental Psychology: An Advanced Textbook.* Hillsdale, N.J., Lawrence Erlbaum, 1984, ch. 1.

[4]*Thus Spoke Zarathustra.* In *The Portable Nietzsche* (trans. and ed. by Walter Kaufmann). New York, Viking Press, 1954.

come weaknesses in the initial formulation, the name of the movement was changed to "logical empiricism," and the initial view was expanded to include theoretical terms. The initial formulation, which uses a referential theory of meaning, would exclude such terms as *electron* because it does not have a referent that can be designated. But by allowing theoretical terms in the second phase, it provided a form of explanation that answers the question of why an event happened by describing the law under which an event has occurred. These laws were in turn explained by their subsumption under more general laws, and all events were finally to be explained from a few basic axioms.

Carl G. Hempel sought to reconstruct scientific laws through use of a deductive network framework.[5] By treating laws as premises in hypothetical statements, deductive explanations are used in which events are subsumed under laws. A *deductive-nomological explanation* was used and it was proposed that existing forms of explanation (e.g., genetic, teleological, historical) are incomplete and need to be translated into deductive nomological form to increase their predictive ability. The explanation is deductive because it uses deductive arguments, and it is nomological because the premises contain general laws. The laws used are called *covering laws* when used as part of the premises and are more general than those laws to be explained. Science is not merely the accumulation of conclusions (e.g., "Behaviors that have been reinforced are likely to be repeated"); it also seeks to understand the arguments used in supporting its conclusions. Hempel and others sought to assess scientific arguments and to reconstruct the reasoning process to develop norms that determine whether a scientist is reasoning correctly. Deductive nomological explanations develop statements of universal form in which a regularity of two events is postulated to occur at all times and places without exception (e.g., if a set of conditions, A, occurs, then C, another set of conditions, occurs as well).

Deductive-nomological explanation is represented in the work of Clark L. Hull, who developed a hypothetico-deductive method in which hypotheses are deduced from postulates and tested empirically.[6] Deficient hypotheses are used as guides to adjust postulates to deduce new

---

[5]Hempel, Carl G. and Oppenheim, Paul: Studies in the logic of explanation. In Brody, Baruch A. (Ed.): *Readings in the Philosophy of Science.* Englewood Cliffs, N.J., Prentice-Hall, 1970, pp. 8–27; Hempel, Carl G.: The logic of functional analysis. In Brodbeck, May (Ed.): *Readings in the Philosophy of Social Science.* New York, Macmillan, 1968, pp. 179–210.

[6]Hull, Clark L.: *A Behavior System.* New Haven, Yale U.P., 1952.

hypotheses and thereby establish a self-correcting system. The system's basic principle is that habit strength increases by reinforcement. The law of acquisition holds that habit strength is gradually built up in increments of habit by contiguous reinforcement of S–R units.

Hull is one of the first psychologists to develop a highly quantified learning theory, and it has proven to be valuable in studying the role of reinforcement in establishing conditioned responses. But the theory expired because of its own excesses by introducing innumerable variables as part of the postulate system.

Research in the social and behavioral sciences is usually not intended to test hypotheses derived from a theoretical network; instead, researchers study a limited number of variables and produce summaries of observed correlations. The findings are empirical generalizations rather than scientific laws. Ernest Nagel used the term *experimental law* for empirical generalization and observed that it can be formulated independently of the theory and it is based on observational evidence that enable the law to survive the demise of the theory.[7] Nagel formulated three essential elements in theory: (1) an abstract calculus that defines the basic notions of the system; (2) a set of rules that assign empirical content to the abstract calculus by relating it to observation and experiment; (3) an interpretation or model that supplies conceptual or visual materials.[8]

A satisfactory model exhibits an analogy with phenomena to be explained in such a manner that there is an identity of structure between aspects of the model and phenomena.[9] Thus there may be an analogy in certain respects between the model and the phenomena (positive analogy), whereas in other respects the model is unlike the phenomena (negative analogy). Atoms, for instance, are like and unlike billiard balls. Models serve a heuristic function by suggesting and guiding research.

Models have been used in many disciplines. Various earlier models can be found in education: the mind as a muscle (formal-discipline theory); the mind as a receptacle or storage bin for knowledge; Rousseau's unfoldment model; Dewey's growth model; the school as a factory, to name a few. Psychology has had its share of influential models: instinct

---

[7]Nagel, Ernest: *The Structure of Science.* New York, Harcourt, Brace & World, 1961.

[8]Ibid., p. 90.

[9]Hesse, Mary B.: The role of models in scientific theory. In Shapera, Dudley (Ed.): *Philosophical Problems in Natural Science.* New York, Macmillan, 1965, pp. 102–09.

as a hydraulic system (Freud); equilibration system (Piaget); the brain as a computer (information-processing approach); mechanism (behaviorism); contextualism (functionalism). Other models that have influenced developmental theory include: homeostasis (W.B. Cannon); evolution (Darwin); humans as machines (Thomas Hobbes); society as an organism (Herbert Spencer).

Returning to the functions of laws, it was noted that Hempel used covering laws as part of the premises for hypothetico-deductive explanation. In contrast, J.S. Mill recommended that the researcher begin with unprejudiced observations of facts and then proceed by inductive inference to the formulations of laws about these facts.[10] Thus a series of evidence reports is inspected and a general statement is inductively inferred from it. Mill believed that induction is based on the principle of the uniformity of nature, which holds that everything has a cause and causal laws are invariant. He also thought that this principle can be established inductively by observing that we have already discovered many empirical laws and therefore generalizations can be made on the basis of them to attain the principle. Mill states that he does not beg the question because the principle was not used in the induction that established it or in the induction leading to the laws from which it was induced.

B.F. Skinner avoids deductive theories and relies on an inductive approach to experimentation. His investigations start with empirical data and proceed tentatively to limited-range generalizations. His positivistic approach is reminiscent of Auguste Comte's positivism, and his inductive method falls within the tradition of Francis Bacon and Mill.

Skinner rejects any method of inquiry that does not depend upon sensory observation. His method proceeds by first clearly identifying the observed data. Then the data are placed in classes, and laws are established to indicate their interrelationships. Finally, a higher and more abstract order of general concepts is developed.

He differs with John B. Watson in limiting the function of his system to description rather than explanation. He seeks to avoid Watson's reductionism by defining concepts in terms of observables rather than reducing them to physiological states. Although private events are not accessible to research, there is no reason to believe that the stimulus from an infected tooth is different from a hot stove. The former can be treated as

---

[10]Mill, John Stuart: *A System of Logic.* London, Routledge, 1879, Book 3.

an inference rather than an observable fact.[11] With the advancement of research techniques, private events will eventually become amenable to scientific investigation. The task of psychology is to determine the relationship between the stimulus controlled by the researcher, the other experimental variables, and the response of the subject.

Logical positivism also relies on induction. Its theory of truth is based on the *verification principle,* which holds that "a statement has meaning only if it is verifiable."[12] But must it be technically possible in the present to verify the statement? Consider the statement, "There is intelligent life in the universe beyond the reach of our most powerful telescopes." Verifying this statement empirically is not possible, but we still know its meaning. This formulation was later changed to the thesis: "A proposition has meaning only if it is possible to confirm it." The conditions are now less stringent. For instance, if there were ten conditions needed to verify a principle and only three had been discovered, then the statement has been confirmed but not verified; all ten conditions would be needed for verification.

If, however, the earlier verification principle was too limited, the confirmation version was too broad because it admitted as meaningful such metaphysical statements as, "Either the sun is shining or the Absolute is imperfect." A more supportable approach was offered by Karl Popper.[13] He seriously questioned the use of induction by logical positivists and others. Theories are not developed by inductive procedures, he said; they begin as imaginative conjectures. Knowledge, then, is not a structure built up by inductive inference from passively received sensations. The process is theoretical and conjectural, a way of putting imaginative questions to the world to see if they can be falsified or refuted. Thus Popper proposed the construction of theories and the attempt to falsify them rather than the logical positivist approach of induction and the verification of propositions. When a hypothesis survives serious attempts to falsify it, it can then be provisionally accepted but never conclusively established (because science is an open system).

But what constitutes falsification? He held that a theory or hypothesis is falsifiable if it is incompatible with some set of basic propositions,

---

[11]Skinner, B.F.: *Science and Human Behavior.* New York, Macmillan, 1953, p. 258.

[12]Schlick, M.: Meaning and verification. *Philosophical Review,* 45: 339–69, 1936; Ayer, A.J.: *Language, Truth, and Logic.* New York, Dover, 1946.

[13]Popper, Karl: *Conjectures and Refutations.* New York, Harper Torchbooks, 1965.

which are propositions that assign some observable physical property to a region of space-time and is accepted by fiat. Not all theories, however, are formulated in a form that is logically inconsistent with basic propositions, as they may have terms standing for unobservables or assign probability to propositions. Those theorists who refuse to accept auxiliary hypotheses or even basic propositions in an attempt to be immune to falsification would not be engaged in scientific procedures.

Growing up in Vienna (though not a member of the Vienna Circle), Popper was interested in Marxism, psychoanalysis, and Adler's individual psychology. One thing he later found that they had in common was their numerous confirmations that "verified" the theories in question. A Marxist would uncover daily confirmation of his theory of history in the newspaper; Freudian analysts would emphasize that their theories were constantly verified by clinical observations; and Popper found in his personal contact with Adler that cases that did not seem to fit his psychology, Adler would reinterpret as inferiority feelings. Popper offers two different cases to illustrate his point: one man pushes a child into the water in an attempt to drown her; another man risks his life to save the child. Each case can be explained with equal ease using Freud's theory or Adler's. For Freud, the first man suffered from repression and the second man had achieved sublimation. According to Adler, the first man suffered from inferiority (a need to prove himself sufficiently to commit a crime) and so did the second man (he had to prove his daring by rescuing the child). Thus there is no behavior that could not be interpreted in terms of either theory; consequently, what ostensibly seems to be the strength of these theories is actually their weakness: that they are not falsifiable or refutable.[14]

Imre Lakatos, a student of Popper who differs somewhat with his mentor, shifted the focus from the hypothesis or conjecture to the research program.[15] The history of science is the history of developing competing research programs. A program is more progressive if it is more comprehensive, if it predicts and explains new facts, and resolves inconsistencies in the old program it replaces.

The need to move beyond theories for a demarcation criterion is because falsificationism does not account for the persistence of theories

---

[14]Ibid., ch. 1.

[15]Lakatos, Imre: Falsification and the methodology of scientific research programmes. In Lakatos, Imre and Musgrave, Alan (Eds.): *Criticism and the Growth of Knowledge.* Cambridge, Cambridge University Press, 1970.

despite disconfirmation. This problem with theories was recognized in Thomas Kuhn's view of normal science.[16] But Kuhn's commitment to the incommensurability of paradigms is too relativistic for Lakatos because one cannot distinguish pseudo-science from real science. Against Kuhn, Lakatos holds that science is a rationally accumulating body of knowledge; against Popper, he claims that its progress is not solely by trial and error. Theories are maintained long after crucial experiments have been devised and conducted because the recognition that the experiment was crucial is a *post hoc* affair. Thus Lakatos believes that reasons can be discerned for the growth of scientific knowledge in the research program. What exactly is a research program? Lakatos lists Newton's gravitational theory, Einstein's relativity theory, Marxism, and Freudianism. Lakatos believes that Marxism and Freudianism are pseudo-scientific because they do not predict novel facts and whatever predictions made have failed to be confirmed. But this criterion is less clear when applied to behaviorism or Keynesian economics.

A shift in thinking became evident in Europe with the influence of hermeneutics. Though hermeneutics can be traced from the seventeenth century in terms of a methodology for interpreting biblical texts, its more modern counterpart emerged in 1894 with such distinctions as Wilhelm Windelband's "nomothetic" and "idiographic" labels to distinguish between natural science's and historical science's approaches to phenomena. Wilhelm Dilthey (1833–1911) was a major opponent of positivism in the human sciences.[17] He argued instead that hermeneutics was essential for understanding human life. Life is human experience from within that occurs within a historical context. Our world consists of value and meaning in which one experiences through perceiving and apprehending. The inner human world is penetrated not by introspection but by interpretation. The sciences explain; human studies seek understanding. *Verstehen* (understanding) designates the operation by which one mind comprehends another mind. Personal and nonconceptual sides of reality are encountered only through understanding. Historically, according to Dilthey, means that humans understand themselves through objectifications in history. He takes a relativist position that history provides world views without fixed standards for determining the superi-

---

[16]Kuhn, Thomas S.: *The Structure of Scientific Revolutions,* 2nd ed. Chicago: U. Chicago Press, 1970.

[17]Ermath, Michael: *William Dilthey: The Critique of Historical Reason.* Chicago, University of Chicago Press, 1978.

ority of any world view. No irreplaceable starting point for understanding exists because every act of understanding is from a particular frame of reference.

Our emphasis is on Dithey's position rather than more recent ones because of his sharp distinctions that highlight the issues. Studies of human development generally have either ignored hermeneutics or have rejected it because of its emphasis on the idiographic rather than nomothetic, its relativism and subjectivity. A notable exception is Martin Packer's work (Chapter 3). An influential contemporary figure who has sought an integration of hermeneutical and empirical modes of inquiry is Jurgen Habermas.

Habermas claims that all knowledge is gained in pursuit of cognitive interests: technical, hermeneutic, and emancipatory.[18] Empirical-analytic sciences seek a technical mastery over nature. Hermeneutics seeks an understanding of rational intersubjective beings by interpretation of purposes, motives, and intentions. Emancipatory interest is concerned with securing freedom from restraint, especially from distorted ideology. Human history, though it expresses subjectivity, is constrained by domination, repression, and ideology. Emancipation, however, can be gained from an analysis of the constraints on cognitive processes. Hermeneutics will show how non-distorting communication is possible. Habermas appeals to the notion of a rational community where false consciousness could be detected because the preconditions that give rise to it can be discussed. Rational communities fully acknowledge human interests and all positions are open to critical evaluation.

In conclusion, theory development is pluralistic, involving inductive, deductive, hermeneutical and eclectic models. Development theory has moved historically from description to prediction and has emphasized explanation. The range of moral development theory encompasses a broad array of diverse systems that compete for followers and, while cognitive models were prominent earlier, pluralism prevails today.

DETERMINISM AND NONDETERMINISM

The problems raised by the issue of determinism and nondeterminism pose salient questions for the explanation of human behavior. *Determinism* is the view that every event has a cause. This should be distinguished

---

[18]Habermas, Jurgen: *Knowledge and Human Interests.* Boston, Beacon Press, 1968.

from *fatalism,* which holds that all events are irrevocably predetermined and cannot be altered in any way by humans, and that the future is beyond human control. The fatalistic view can be found in Calvinistic predestination. Determinism can be divided into hard and soft determinism. *Hard determinism* holds that human desires, thoughts, and actions are "determined" by prior causes over which humans have no control. Children do not choose their genetic makeup, the culture they grow up in, or their family environment. Since individuals have no control over these factors, they cannot be responsible for their original character or control their desires. "We can choose in accordance with our desires, but we are not free to desire."[19] In contrast, *soft determinism* states that all events are caused, but some events and causes originate with human beings. Hard determinists object to this view on grounds that if events were traced back far enough, they would originate outside of the individual's control.

Both Freud and Skinner are hard determinists. Freud's psychology is thoroughly mechanistic in the best of the nineteenth century tradition of science. Events and entities are related to one another externally rather than organically. The self, personality, consciousness are mere epiphenomena or by-products of the pleasure-principle. The adjustments are mechanically based on laws of association which explain the behavior of the whole in terms of the parts without attempting to show how the parts come together to make the whole. How the parts affect other parts through mechanical laws is never clearly explained. The parts are viewed as antecedent to the whole which somehow constitutes a derived product. Biological research does not support the position that parts are antecedent to structures and are primarily in relation to the whole. In fact, the opposite is held to be the case.

Relation in Freud's mechanistic position is a causal determinism that proceeds in a linear fashion by relating every present act to antecedent acts beginning in infancy. Humans, in the scheme of things, are not free to act; a hard determinism causes their behavior, and what humans become is a result of early childhood influences.

Skinner's operant behaviorism is a hard determinism. The individual is a reactive (rather than a proactive) organism that responds to and is conditioned by the contingencies of reinforcement in the environment,

---

[19]Hospers, John: *Human Conduct.* New York: Harcourt, Brace, Jovanovich, 1961, p. 508.

which would explain both desirable and undesirable behavior and do away with the need to appeal to individual responsibility.

Skinner believed that to make people happy, we need to make better use of the reinforcers we already have. And any new techniques of control should not involve punishment. Since we are always under the control of environment, anyway, and since control in a utopian plan benefits the person under control, the individual need not fear control. Control can arise from accident or design, but it would be better to design it. As behavioral technology advances, it can be used to design cultures that reinforce desirable behavior. The most significant problem, then, for moral development theory is that hard determinism rules out human choice and individual responsibility.

In contrast, Piaget's and Kohlberg's developmental theories can be classified as a form of soft determinism, which recognizes causality and multiple causal forces, including one's own decisions. Both Piaget and Kohlberg oppose traditional empiricist and nativist philosophies of the mind. They oppose empiricist psychologies for overemphasizing external determinants of behavior and viewing the mind as a *tabula rasa*, and nativist psychologies for overemphasizing the degree of fixity in human nature by heredity. Thus the need for psychology to be cognitive is necessitated by the shortcoming of empiricism, and the need to be developmental stems from nativism's shortcomings.[20]

Another theory that likely fits into soft determinism is John W. Berry's ecological model (in Chapter 5). He sought to avoid weaknesses of previous cross-cultural models by treating each of the modeled relationships as probabilistic and by employing feedback relations for most of the elements in the model. Cultural and behavioral variables are considered to be adapting to ecology; adaptive relationships are probabilistic, and are subject to empirical testing.

The position of nondeterminism maintains that people are autonomous and responsible for much of what they do. It is argued that this is known from our own experiences in making decisions and acting in which the ultimate cause is the agent. Individuals can choose actions other than those they undertake.

An example of nondeterminism is Martin Packer's hermeneutical approach (in Chapter 3). He posits social action as organized semantically by the meanings people find in social events and action rather than in

---

[20]Flanagan, Owen: *The Science of the Mind,* 2nd ed. Cambridge, MIT Press, 1984, ch. 5.

terms of material causation or logical necessity. Human actions can be understood in a variety of ways, but social exchanges are best understood through an inductive approach.

Indeterminism, as a metaphysical theory, holds that some events cannot be explained by being subsumed under universal laws, and cannot be predicted because of chance and spontaneity in the universe. As an ethical doctrine, a rational being has freedom of the will to choose without being compelled; therefore, ethical choices are not caused by antecedent events.

A leading representative of the free will view is William James, who sought in his pragmatism to combat monism and dualism with his theory of pluralism, which holds that the world is composed of many things. The world is not entirely unified; there is sufficient looseness in it to keep the future open and to allow individual freedom.

But James admits that psychology, for scientific purposes, can claim determinism. Yet ethics makes a stronger counter-claim that our wills are free. Thus, the deterministic assumptions of psychology are merely methodological and provisional.[21] Determinism fits best with the scientific approach, whereas free will accords with our moral, legal, and political practices. But since the latter is the most comprehensively, widely-shared life form, then James chooses free will.

A most serious problem, however, for James and other free will advocates is that if an act is not caused, then no one caused it, including those we may want to designate as "moral persons." Thus, all human acts are beyond moral responsibility and praise, blame, reward and punishment cannot be assigned. Indeterminism, therefore, is not only empirically dubious but undermines moral ascriptions and does not support the argument for human freedom, as it only assures accident and chance, not freedom. James would have been better served by choosing soft determinism or nondeterminism.

MORALITY AND IMMORALITY

What does it mean to be moral? Are the claims about moral behavior in moral development theories always about such behavior or in some cases misclassified? If so, what is the import of such errors for moral

---

[21]James, William: *Principles of Psychology.* Cambridge, Harvard U.P., 1976, p. 1177.

development theory? To speak intelligently about moral development, is a theory of immorality also needed?

The notion of immorality is a complex one because it involves understanding what it means to be moral. One way that this idea can be made clear is by distinguishing certain basic terms. First of all, the terms "mores" and "morality" should be distinguished. By *mores* is meant the fixed morally-binding customs of a particular group. Mores vary considerably cross-culturally and throughout human history, ranging from the noblest behavior to the approval of slavery, infanticide, burning infidels at the stake, genocide and other heinous practices. In contrast, *morality* is a system of conduct based on moral principles. That which is *moral*, therefore, relates to principles of right conduct in behavior; the behavior conforms to accepted principles of what is considered right, virtuous, or just.

The application of a taxonomy may better conceptualize immorality. R.D. Milo has explicated a taxonomy of immorality in terms of six types that are classified according to three principle sources of immoral conduct.[22] The three sources are: bad preferences (or values); lack of concern for the interest of others; and lack of rational self-control.

The first source—bad preferences (or values)—could be conceived either as perverse wickedness or preferential wickedness. An agent who holds immoral principles and believes that acting on these principles is the right thing to do would be an example of *perverse wickedness*. In contrast, the agent who does what is wrong because s(he) prefers some other objective than the avoidance of moral wrongdoing is a case of *preferential wickedness*. In other words, in the case of perverse wickedness the agent believes the acts that flow from immoral principles are either morally required or, at least, morally permissible; whereas the conception of preferential wickedness, though the agent recognizes what s(he) is doing is wrong, s(he) nonetheless prefers the attainment of a certain objective rather than the avoidance of wrongdoing.

The second source of immoral conduct is a lack of concern for the interests of others and consists of amorality and moral indifference. *Amorality* is where the agent neither believe that what s(he) is doing is wrong nor believes that it is right; in other words, the agent has no moral principles in regard to the acts disputed. *Moral indifference* involves

---

[22]Milo, R.D.: *Immorality,* Princeton, NJ, Princeton University Press, 1984.

doing what is morally wrong because it promotes a desired objective and the agent is totally unmoved by its wrongness.

A lack of rational self-control is the third source of immoral conduct and consists of moral negligence and moral weakness. *Moral negligence* involves the failure to prevent emotions and desires from distorting one's judgment. In the case of *moral weakness,* the agent allows emotions and desires to prevent acting on one's judgment. Thus, with instances of moral negligence the agent is ignorant that the conduct in question is in violation of one's own moral principles and thereby mistakenly assumes that the action is right. In contrast, an agent of a morally weak act prefers to avoid wrongdoing, but the desire to engage in the act is stronger than the desire to avoid wrongdoing.

The taxonomy can be readily applied to moral development theory in terms of the three principal sources of immoral conduct. Bad preferences or values, the first source, can be found in Adler's Individual Psychology. For Adler, such undesirable preferences or values arise when individuals are not motivated by social interest. Egocentric strivings for power would be viewed by Adler as counterproductive to an individual's value system and a neurotic manifestation in behavior. One should instead value empathy for others, communal feeling, and impersonality.

The second type of immorality is a lack of concern for others' interests. Three different theories illustrate this type. Gilligan shows that in acting morally, women especially use a language of care and responsibility that involves being there, listening, helping and understanding in which one does not turn away from need. A second position is Martin Hoffman's theory of empathy and social cognition. He finds that sensitivity to the rights and welfare of others, especially when in conflict with one's own interests, are central features of the moral domain. How does one act when s(he) finds another person in a needful state? In other situations can one curb the tendency to act in harmful ways against someone? Piaget's moral development theory is a third response to this type of immorality. Piaget sees the young child as subscribing to a heterono-mous morality and inhibited by a lengthy period of egocentrism charac-terized by a relative inability to separate components of internal and external reality. This prevents the child from placing himself (Piaget's subjects were boys) in the viewpoint of another person. Thus to become moral the young must move beyond the egocentrism period.

Lack of self-control is the third source of immorality and examples can be found in several theories. Social learning theory holds that the young child lacks control over behavior and tends to interpret positive and negative outcomes as a result of external rather than internal factors. But the child begins to assume personal responsibility with the growth of cognitive and behavioral competence. The child develops standards of self-control in three distinctive ways. One is by external monitoring and intervention by authority figures when the child may do personal harm to others or oneself. Second, the child may anticipate external reward or punishment by those who can reinforce or withhold reinforcement. Third, the maturing child may reach the point where internal control is dominant. Nevertheless, the child continues to accept parental standards as one's own because of potential feelings of guilt, shame, and self-derogation should the child violate parental judgments.[23]

In a hermeneutical approach, Martin Packer (in Chapter 3) used a modified version of the Prisoner's Dilemma game in which team members agreed to play cooperatively, but in 4 out of 10 sessions the winners broke the agreement. The winning team's behavior is an example of moral negligence, as they were unaware that their actions would appear immoral to the losing team. After a period of impasse characterized by certitude and egocenteredness, issues were more thoroughly addressed and shifted from a transgressor-transgressed relationship to different ways of understanding events.

The problems of self-control in psychoanalysis is that the ego has to balance the id and the super ego. A Freudian explanation of children who lack sufficient conscience is the failure to develop a super ego, thereby permitting the id to dominate and run roughshod over the ego. Freud believes that a substantial amount of repression is needed to balance id impulses with cultural demands. Sublimation, a form of repression, is a defense mechanism that transforms id impulses into more socially acceptable behavior. Freud calls upon humans to sublimate aggressive instincts so that civilization can obtain mastery over the dangerous love of aggression. Sublimation serves to build culture in the form of religion, literature, art, and the like.[24] In conclusion, it can be seen that each moral development theory needs to state a position on immorality for a more complete conceptualization, rather than leaving it to the reader to infer it, perhaps erroneously.

Are the claims about morality in moral development theory always

[23]Sears, R.R., Maccoby, E.E., Levin, H.: *Patterns of Child Rearing.* Evanston, IL, Row, Peterson, 1957.

[24]Freud, Sigmund: *Civilization and Its Discontents.* New York, Norton, 1961.

about such behavior or in some cases misclassified? That would depend upon one's conception of moral decision and action. In order to say that someone in a particular instance acted morally is meaningful only when an act is voluntary, intentional, based on moral principles, and considers the good of everyone likely to be affected by the act. It must be voluntary rather than coerced, intentional rather than accidental, based on sound reasons for the moral principle used, employ appropriate principles for the situation, and the agent considers the good of everyone affected by the act rather than the agent's own good exclusively.

The agent must be able to be held responsible for the act before praise or blame can be ascribed or sanctions imposed. If the person is coerced, then responsibility cannot be assigned to that person; or if the individual accidentally commits an undesirable act, less responsibility can be assigned than if the act is intentional (though the person can be reprimanded for being careless in acts with untoward effects and not be given credit for accidental acts that have beneficial effects). As for moral principles, obviously someone who impulsively performs an act that has a beneficial effect on others cannot be considered to be demonstrating good moral character as would someone whose actions are clearly guided by moral principles that are not arbitrarily chosen and are applied correctly to different situations. Agents should consider how their acts affect others, the possible benefits derived and the harm imposed. By "harm" is meant an injury to something in which a person has a genuine stake. Those things in which one has a genuine stake are both relatively permanent (one's health and security) and temporary (property that one plans to sell).

Some other grounds on which morality is ascribed are open to question. Legal obedience is a large topic and cannot be pursued far here,[25] yet not only is legal compliance to unjust laws not moral but legal compliance strictly on the basis of fear is not a moral motive. The proposition that humans will be rewarded if moral and punished if they are not does not base choices on moral grounds. Some may claim that this world is unjust and reward will come in the next world. But this is clearly a non sequitur, for the mere fact that this world is unjust does not prove either that there is another world or that it is just. Moreover, to act from fear of

---

[25]See: Welch, D. Don (Ed.): *Law and Morality.* Philadelphia, Fortress Press, 1987; Greenawalt, Kent: *Conflicts of Law and Morality.* New York, Clarendon Press, 1987.

God's punishment and a desire for reward in the next world is to base morality on self-interest.

Some believe that a moral act must be based on conscience. The annals of history, however, are filled with examples of appeals to conscience by the power elite to rationalize unjust acts. Conscience, logically speaking, does not tell one what to do. A decision to do something does not follow logically from a command to do it. The function of conscience is that of "advising, exhorting, or commanding, not of deciding or choosing."[26] The process of deciding and choosing evolves from a reflective assessment of social conditions based on relevant evidence evaluated according to one's system of values.

The above view of acting morally differs with some theories presented. Martin Hoffman holds that a moral issue arises when people's goals, plans, or expectations are in conflict. Sensitivity to the rights and welfare of others, especially when they conflict with one's own interest, are central features of the moral domain. Gilligan, on the other hand, finds care concerns the focus of a moral perspective. Our position is more restrictive and hierarchical than Hoffman's and leaves Gilligan's central concern implicit. What our position does is to rule out as moral behavior many features of the various theories: the activities of the Freudian super ego, Piaget's heteronomous morality, Kohlberg's first four stages, Loevinger's first six stages, and Kurtines' first two levels. The earlier stages are premoral but influenced in varying degrees by socialization and may possibly be prerequisite to moral decision making and action. If this is so, then the formulation of these theories needs to be reconceived. In any case, what we have seen is that the moral life is complex and demanding but essential if persons are to become fully-functioning members of society.

---

[26]Nowell-Smith, P.H.: *Ethics.* Baltimore, Penguin, 1954, p. 260.

BIBLIOGRAPHY

This is a minimum working bibliography of essential materials. Readers needing additional references should consult footnotes.

Adler, Alfred: *Co-operation Between the Sexes.* Ansbacher, Heinz L. and Rowena R. (Eds.) New York, Norton, 1978.

Adler, Alfred: *Social Interest: Challenge to Mankind.* New York, Capricorn, 1964.

Baltes, Paul B.: Reese, Hayne W.; Nesselroade, John R.: *Life-Span Developmental Psychology: Introduction to Research Methods.* Monterey, CA, Brooks/Cole, 1977.

Bandura, Albert: *Social Foundations of Thought and Action.* Englewood Cliffs, NJ, Prentice-Hall, 1986.

Bandura, Albert: *Social Learning Theory.* New York, Prentice-Hall, 1977.

Berndt, Thomas J. and Zigler, Edward F.: Developmental psychology. In Kimble, Gregory A. and Schlesinger, Kurt (Eds.): *Topics in the History of Psychology.* Hillsdale, NJ, Lawrence Erlbaum, 1985, vol. 2, ch. 4.

Berry, John W., et al (Eds.): *Cross-Cultural Psychology: Research and Applications.* New York, Cambridge U.P., 1992.

Berry, John W.: *Human Ecology and Cognitive Style.* Beverly Hills, CA, Sage, 1976.

Bowen, Howard R.: *Investment in Learning.* San Francisco, Jossey-Bass, 1977.

Blum, Lawrence A.: *Friendship, Altruism and Morality.* London, Routledge and Kegan Paul, 1980.

Chickering, Arthur W.: *Education and Identity.* San Francisco, Jossey-Bass, 1969.

Cirillo, Leonard and Wapner, Seymour (Eds.): *Value Presuppositions in Theories of Human Development* Hillsdale, NJ, Lawrence Erlbaum, 1986.

DeVitis, Joseph L.: Cooperation and social equality in childhood: Adlerian and Piagetian lessons. *Journal of Research and Development in Education,* 17:23, 1984.

Dixon, Roger A. and Lerner, Richard M.: A history of systems in developmental psychology. In Bornstein, Marc H. and Lamb, Michael E. (Eds.): *Developmental Psychology: An Advanced Textbook.* Hillsdale, NJ: Lawrence Erlbaum, 1984, ch. 1.

Dreikurs, Rudolf and Soltz, Vicki: *Children: The Challenge.* New York, Hawthorn, 1964.

Dreikurs, Rudolf: *Social Equality: The Challenge of Today.* Chicago, Regenery, 1971.

Durkheim, Emile: *Moral Education.* New York, Free Press, 1925/1961.

Erikson, Erik H.: *Childhood and Society,* 2nd ed. New York, Norton, 1963.

Erikson, Erik H.: *Insight and Responsibility.* New York, Norton, 1964.

Feldman, Kenneth A. and Newcomb, Theodore M.: *The Impact of College on Students,* San Francisco, Jossey-Bass, 1969.

Fowler, James W.: *Stages of Faith: The Psychology of Human Development and the Quest for Meaning.* San Francisco, Harper & Row, 1981.

Garrod, Andrew (Ed.): *Approaches to Moral Development.* New York, Teachers College, 1993.

Gilligan, Carol: *In a Different Voice: Psychological Theory and Women's Development.* Cambridge, Harvard U.P., 1982.

Gilligan, Carol, et al. (Eds.): *Mapping the Moral Domain.* Cambridge, Harvard U.P., 1988.

Hartshorne, Hugh and May, M.A.: *Studies in the Nature of Character.* New York, Macmillan, 1928–30, 3 vols.

Havighurst, Robert J.: *Human Development and Education.* New York, McKay, 1953.

Jacob, Philip E.: *Changing Values in College.* New York, Harper, 1957.

Jacob, Jolan: *The Psychology of Jung,* K.W. Bash (Tr.) New Haven, Yale U.P., 1943.

Jacoby, Russell: *Social Amnesia: A Critique of Contemporary Psychology from Adler to Laing.* Boston, Beacon, 1976.

Jung, Carl: *Collected Papers of C.G. Jung.* R.F.C. Hull (Tr.), New York, Pantheon, 1954.

Jung, Carl: *Psychological Types — Or the Psychology of Individuation.* H.G. Baynes (Tr.). London, Kegan Paul, 1923.

Kardiner, Abram: *The Individual and His Society: The Psychodynamics of Primitive Social Organization.* New York, Columbia U.P., 1939.

Keniston, Kenneth: *Young Radicals: Notes on Committed Youth.* New York, Harcourt, Brace, & World, 1968.

Keniston, Kenneth: *Youth and Dissent: The Rise of a New Opposition.* New York, Harcourt Brace Jovanovich, 1971.

Kohlberg, Lawrence: *The Philosophy of Moral Development: Moral Stages and the Idea of Justice.* New York, Harper & Row, 1981.

Kohlberg, Lawrence: *The Psychology of Moral Development:* San Francisco, Harper & Row, 1984.

Kurtines, William M. and Gewirtz, Jacob L. (Eds.): *Handbook of Moral Behavior and Development.* Hillsdale, NJ, Lawrence Erlbaum, 1991, 3 vols.

Kurtines, William M. and Gewirtz, Jacob L.: *Moral Development Through Social Interaction.* New York, Wiley, 1987.

Kurtines, William M. and Gewirtz, Jacob L. (Eds.): *Morality, Moral Behavior, and Moral Development.* New York, Wiley, 1984.

Levinson, Daniel J., et al.: *The Seasons of a Man's Life.* New York, Knopf, 1978.

Loevinger, Jane and Wessler, Ruth: *Measuring Ego Development.* San Francisco, Jossey-Bass, 1970, vol. 1.

Marcuse, Herbert: *Eros and Civilization: A Philosophical Inquiry into Freud.* New York, Vintage, 1962.

Miller, Patricia H.: *Theories of Developmental Psychology.* San Francisco, W.H. Freeman, 1983.

Modgil, S. and Modgil, C. (Eds.): *Lawrence Kohlberg: Consensus and Controversy.* Philadelphia, Falmer Press, 1986.

Packer, Martin J.: *The Structure of Moral Action: A Hermeneutic Study of Moral Conflict.* Basel, Karger, 1985.

Pascarella, Ernest T.: College environmental influences on learning and cognitive development: A critical review and synthesis. In Smart, John (Ed.): *Higher Education: Handbook of Theory and Research.* New York: Agathon, 1985, vol. 1, pp. 1–61.

Perry, William G.: *Forms of Intellectual and Ethical Development in the College Years: A Scheme.* New York, Holt, Rinehart and Winston, 1970.

Peters, R.S.: *Psychology and Ethical Development.* London, Allen & Unwin, 1974.

Piaget, Jean: *The Moral Judgement of the Child.* New York, Collier, 1932/1962.

Poster, Mark: *Critical Theory of the Family.* New York, Seabury, 1980.

Rieff, Philip: *The Mind of the Moralist.* Garden City, NY, Doubleday, 1959.

Roazen, Paul: *Erik H. Erikson: The Power and Limits of a Vision.* New York, Free, 1976.

Rosen, Hugh: *The Development of Sociomoral Knowledge: A Cognitive-Structural Approach.* New York, Columbia U.P., 1980.

Salkind, Neil J.: *Theories of Human Development.* New York, D. Van Nostrand, 1981.

Strachey, J. (Ed.): *The Standard Edition of the Complete Psychological Works of Sigmund Freud.* London, Hogarth, 1953–1966.

Van Geert, Paul: *Theory Building in Developmental Psychology.* New York, North-Holland, 1986.

Way, Lewis: *Adler's Place in Psychology: An Exposition of Individual Psychology.* New York, Collier, 1962.

Wolman, Benjamin B. (Ed.): *Handbook of Developmental Psychology.* Englewood Cliffs, NJ, Prentice-Hall, 1982.

INDEX

151